"Knowing David Ireland personally, as I have since he began Christ Church, I have seen the outworking of this book in the life and growth of the man and the church. In a day when there have been many books on faith, this volume, which applies faith to everyday life, is outstanding. Because David has walked the journey himself, believers, both young and old, can gain new and fresh insights to the life of faith that produces miracles. Everyone is called, from time to time, to step out of the boat. Knowing where the 'hidden rocks' are will make walking on water a rich experience. This book is a must for all Christians, whether they are new believers or have been on the way for many years, because walking on water is not a once-in-a-lifetime event, it is a lifestyle."

Paul Johansson, president, Elim Bible Institute

"This is a clear, careful, and concise dissection of faith. The notion of faith walk and faith talk has been so bastardized by the Christian community that many believers and unbelievers are faithless. Dr. Ireland takes us on a biblically responsible analysis of faith that works within the context of the Christlike life. I encourage each reader to apply this understanding so that faith can grow in every area of life."

Jacqueline E. McCullough, pastor,
The Gathering at Beth Rapha, Mahwah, New Jersey

"David Ireland's book *Why Drown When You Can Walk on Water?* spoke right to my heart. My faith was wonderfully built. It is a book that I will want to read again, it's that good."

Dr. Che Ahn, senior pastor, Harvest Rock Church, Pasadena, California

"This book should help David Ireland's ministry to go from being one of the church's best-kept secrets to one of its best-loved stories."

Leonard Sweet, E. Stanley Jones Professor of Evangelism,
Drew University

"The miracle of *Why Drown When You Can Walk on Water?* is resurrection. Well-known Bible stories are raised to new life as master storyteller David Ireland pulls important lessons of faith out of so many wonderful stories and real-life illustrations. His rich pastoral heart comes through these teachings. Like me, you may find yourself wishing you were part of his congregation, as you sense that it really does matter to Dr. Ireland that you grow mighty in faith.

"While a fish may be too close to the water to teach us about hydraulics, David's lessons of faith are all the more valuable precisely because he does live the life of faith that he preaches. You will find that the elusive spiritual ideal of faith becomes daily-life practical, as you see how you can incorporate the principles you learn in each chapter."

David E. Schroeder, president, Nyack College

WHY
DROWN
WHEN YOU CAN
WALK *on* WATER?

WHY DROWN

WHEN YOU CAN WALK *on* WATER?

Applying Faith to Real Life

David D. Ireland, Ph.D.

BakerBooks
Grand Rapids, Michigan

© 2004 by David D. Ireland, Ph.D.

Published by Baker Books
a division of Baker Publishing Group
P.O. Box 6287, Grand Rapids, MI 49516-6287
www.bakerbooks.com

Printed in the United States of America

Published in association with the literary agency of Alive Communications, Inc., 7680 Goddard Street, Suite 200, Colorado Springs, Colorado 80920.

Library of Congress Cataloging-in-Publication Data
Ireland, David, 1961–
    Why drown when you can walk on water? : applying faith to real life / David D. Ireland.
        p.   cm.
    Includes bibliographical references.
    ISBN 0-8010-6497-X (pbk.)
    1. Christian life. I. Title.
BV4501.3.I74 2004
248.4—dc22   2004009759

CONTENTS

INTRODUCTION

A pastor was hired by a church, and the youth leader and music director took him fishing so they could spend some time getting to know one another. They rowed the boat out on the water, found a good spot, and reached for their poles. "Oops," the music director said, "we left the fishing poles on the bank." The pastor said, "No problem, I'll row back to shore."

"That's not necessary," the music director said, and he got out of the boat, walked across the surface of the water to the riverbank, grabbed the poles, and walked back.

The pastor, needless to say, was awestruck. A few minutes later the youth leader asked for the bait.

"Oops," the music director said, "we left the bait on shore." This time the youth director said, "No problem," and hopped out of the boat, walked across the surface of the water to the river's edge, grabbed the bait, and walked back.

Again the pastor was awestruck. The men baited their hooks and began to fish. Before long the youth director asked for the sandwiches. Again the music director said, "Oops, we left them on shore." He turned to his new boss

9

and said, "Pastor, would you mind going to shore and getting the sandwiches?"

Not wanting to be shown up by his staff members, the pastor stammered for a moment and then said, "Sure." He took one step out of the boat and immediately sank to the bottom of the river. The music director looked at the youth leader and said, "When he comes back up, will you show him where the stepping-stones are?"

The irony of this story is that when someone knows where the stepping-stones are, it seems as if he or she actually is walking on water. This book is intended to show you how to walk on water by pointing out the hidden stepping-stones of faith.

As I write this introduction our congregation is preparing to move from an ornate, 25,000-square-foot historical cathedral to a 107-acre campus. The magnitude of this project is stretching me in ways I never could have imagined. With so much at stake, I often find myself pondering many questions: Can the church handle the financial responsibility of managing a campus? Will all five thousand members make the transition to the new location? Will the presence of the Holy Spirit manifest itself as powerfully in the new setting as in times past? These questions are among the many that help me turn my faith toward God's abilities.

The Bible leaves no doubt on this one point: Without faith it is impossible to please God (Heb. 11:6). I suspect that one of the reasons you are reading this book is that an unfulfilled promise of God is gnawing at your heart. Your desire to apprehend that promise may be challenging you to exercise faith and even to grow your faith muscles during this period.

One of the best Bible stories to demonstrate faith is the invitation Jesus gave Peter to walk on the water (Matt. 14:22–33). The focal point states:

When the disciples saw him walking on the lake, they were terrified. "It's a ghost," they said, and cried out in fear.

But Jesus immediately said to them: "Take courage! It is I. Don't be afraid."

"Lord, if it's you," Peter replied, "tell me to come to you on the water."

"Come," he said.

Then Peter got down out of the boat, walked on the water and came toward Jesus. But when he saw the wind, he was afraid and, beginning to sink, cried out, "Lord, save me!"

Immediately Jesus reached out his hand and caught him. "You of little faith," he said, "why did you doubt?"

Matthew 14:26–31

Somewhere between three and six o'clock in the morning, Jesus decided to join his disciples by walking on the water toward their boat. Uncertain as to what they were really seeing, the frightened disciples cried out in fear, thinking it was a ghost. Once Jesus announced who he was, Peter insisted that Jesus should cause him to walk on the water too. Jesus approved the request. Interestingly enough, Peter walked for a short while on the water until he allowed fear to grip his heart, causing him to sink. Jesus's take on the whole episode was that Peter's doubt nullified his faith. Jesus wanted Peter to succeed in walking on the water. I believe he feels the same way about *your* present and future circumstances, those that call for a sincere use

11

of faith. Can't you hear Jesus in the background encouraging you? He's saying, "Go ahead, walk on water!"

⌒

In writing this book, I wanted to impart a few lessons I've learned as I've worked at growing in my faith. Some of the lessons come from personal experience, some from the Bible, and some from observing the faith of others. As you read, I hope you will take away these four objectives:

1. To Know How to Weather the Storms of Life

All of us will face storms in our lives. Some of us grow in faith by learning to trust God in the daily circumstances of life. Others learn the lessons of faith by riding out one storm after another. Either way, how we respond in the midst of these difficulties determines whether we become bitter or better.

2. To Get a Clearer Perspective of God's Purpose in Your Life

God is as concerned with the growth of your faith as he is with the blessings that faith brings—perhaps even more so. That fact, in itself, should give you a new perspective on the various trials God allows you to experience. How important to God is the growth of your faith? The apostle Peter wrote, "The proof of your faith" is "more precious than gold" (1 Pet. 1:7 NASB). Gold was the principal element used to make currency in those days. Kings hoarded gold during their lives, and the Egyptian pharaohs demanded that it be buried with them upon their death. Peter says the *proof* of your faith is more precious than gold. Thus, you should see your faith as precious, a perspective that will lay the foundation for achieving God's purpose for your life.

3. To Keep Faith Growing

Scripture says, "Without faith it is impossible to please God" (Heb. 11:6). God is just as concerned that we grow in faith as in wisdom, knowledge, and holiness. After Lee Iacocca was fired from Ford Motor Company, he was offered the job as head of Chrysler. Things looked so dismal at Chrysler that Iacocca decided not to take the job, saying to his wife, "I don't think anyone could turn this company around." Mrs. Iacocca replied, "I'm sure Mr. Ford will be glad to hear that."[1] That comment changed Iacocca's mind. Of course, you know what happened. He took the job and performed one of the most miraculous business comebacks in history. To keep faith growing, you must keep accepting the challenges God and life present to you.

4. To Possess by Faith the Promises of God

Hebrews 6:12 tells us to be "imitators of those who through faith and patience inherit the promises" (NASB). Sometimes it takes a great deal of persistence and a perseverance of faith to inherit a promise from God. As you will see in chapter 1, I learned this lesson early on in my walk with the Lord. The biblical instruction offered to believers is that God's promises are appropriated through faith. In essence, faith is a key to unlock, open, and access God's promises.

As you read *Why Drown When You Can Walk on Water?* my greatest hope is that you will be made divinely discontent to remain where you are in your walk with Christ. I pray that you will be inspired and encouraged to grow in faith, that you will make it your highest goal to know God more intimately and to possess his promises by faith. In other words, it's time to walk on water.

one

THE DAY BEFORE
THE MIRACLES

Have you ever wondered what Peter was doing *the day before* he walked on water? In other words, what paved the way for the miracle?

Analyzing Peter's perspective helps us form a psychological picture behind his failed attempt to maintain buoyancy. This diagnosis will help us formulate a mental strategy for achieving the miracles we need from God. I am a firm believer in the value of a constructive reprimand. In Peter's case, Jesus's corrective words "You of little faith, . . . why did you doubt?" (Matt. 14:31) were chock-full of instruction. If you fully understand and heed them, you can establish a faith orientation that will capture all of the miracles God wants to perform in your life.

Matthew 14:31 establishes the point that doubt is the opposite of faith. In fact, the Greek word for doubt is *distazo* (pronounced dis-tad´-zo), which means "to waver in opinion," "to hesitate," or "to be uncertain." *Distazo* is a figurative word that conveys a person standing at a fork in the road, uncertain as to which direction to choose. The word also captures the idea of a scale teetering back and forth repeatedly because the items on both sides are of almost the same weight. In essence Jesus was asking Peter, "Why did you teeter back and forth regarding your ability to walk on the water? Why were you indecisive about what direction to take when you came to the fork in the road?" Jesus's question was not meant to insult or embarrass Peter in front of the other disciples; rather, it was intended to use Peter's faux pas as a teaching point to explain the essentials of faith. If Peter had adopted a faith perspective beforehand, a powerful miracle would have transpired on the lake that night—he too would have walked on water. Understanding the meaning of faith is a prerequisite to achieving great exploits of faith.

Three Ingredients of Faith

A technical definition of faith, along with the various forms the word takes in the Bible, will be explored later in this chapter. For now, I would like to examine the components of faith used to appropriate God's promises. We will then explore questions like these: How can we avoid the errors associated with misguided faith? Is using faith the same as using positive thinking?

In Hebrews 11:1 we learn that "faith is being sure of what we hope for and certain of what we do not see." The writer is telling us that everything about faith encompasses certainty, which embodies three areas—knowledge, belief, and assent. The word *certainty* as used in the New International Version is the Greek word *elenchos* (pronounced el´-eng-khos), which means "proof," "conviction," and "evidence." Although the person employing faith has an internal assurance of the things hoped for, this verse does not imply, nor can it be interpreted to mean, that the believing person can prove to others the reality of the unseen things he or she hopes for.

According to the eminent Greek scholar Gerhard Kittel, by adding the term *hope for* to the word *certain*, the writer of Hebrews conveys that "the inner right of resting on the thing hoped for is established" to the believer.[1] God gives an internal resolve, a confidence to the believer that it is right to rest in the thing being hoped for.

To have confidence, you must first have knowledge about the thing being hoped for. Next, you must believe in the knowledge you possess. And finally, you must act on that belief in order to complete the expression of faith. This is where the word *assent* comes in. Assent is "to concur," "to agree," or "to act on the thing believed." Thus, the meaning of faith could be illustrated through the equation: knowledge + belief + assent = *faith*.

For a working example of how these three components integrate to form faith, I would like to modernize the language and embellish an illustration Charles Haddon Spurgeon used in his sermon titled "Faith," which he preached to his congregation in the famous Surrey Hall of London in the 1800s.[2]

Imagine a young boy caught in the bedroom of a second-floor apartment that's on fire. The boy tries to open the door to his bedroom with the intention of racing through the apartment's front door to safety. However, when he touches the doorknob, it's scorching hot, and smoke begins seeping under his door.

Alarmed, he runs to his bedroom window and opens it with the intent to jump. Faced with the prospect of landing facedown on the concrete pavement, he reconsiders. In a panic-stricken voice he screams for help to the crowd gathering below. A strong man steps from among the onlookers and encourages the boy to jump.

"I'll catch you, son," he says. "Jump!"

Upon hearing the strong man's claim, the boy receives *knowledge*. But this knowledge still isn't faith.

"Help! Help!" the screaming boy cries out even louder.

"Jump, I'll catch you!" assures the strong man. "Don't be afraid, jump!"

Upon further consideration of the man's claims, the boy now *believes* that the big man can catch him. But even his knowledge of and belief in the strong man's assertions do not translate into faith. Once again he moves away from the window.

A few seconds later, the boy goes over to the window a third time screaming for help. "Jump, son, I'll catch you. Don't worry, I'll catch you!" yells the strong man.

This time the boy *assents* to (acts on) his knowledge of, and belief in, the strong man's words by leaping out of the window

18

into his arms. That is faith. The boy assented to what he had knowledge and belief about. The three together form faith.

A friend of mine told me about how she was trusting God by faith to start a car-washing business. I asked her if she knew how much this kind of business cost and whether she had done any research about how to run such an enterprise. When she responded that she didn't know the cost and had done no research, I encouraged her to obtain *knowledge* so that she would have a foundation for her faith. A few weeks later, I asked about her research. "Oh, that," she said. "I found out that it's too expensive for my blood." This remark showed me right away that she was never using biblical faith about running a car wash. Biblical faith is comprised of knowledge, belief, and assent. Having one or two of the items in place does not amount to faith. You need all three.

Take a moment right now to consider the areas in which you have been trying to apply faith. Have you applied all three ingredients? If one or two of the ingredients are missing, this is a great time to pause from your reading and get with the Lord. In prayer, ask the Lord to give you access to the pertinent knowledge you need or the assurance to believe the promises written in his Word. Or seek him for the courage to assent to what you know and believe already. Joy in walking by faith is the end result—obtaining the promises of God, all of them.

What Faith Is Not

Positive thinking should not be considered in conflict with faith or Scripture *if* it is within a biblical framework.

James instructs us on how faith requests should be *positively* voiced in prayer:

> But when he asks, he must believe and not doubt, because he who doubts is like a wave of the sea, blown and tossed by the wind. That man should not think he will receive anything from the Lord; he is a double-minded man, unstable in all he does.
>
> James 1:6–8

Prayer must be approached in a believing, positive manner. The person seeking an answer from God must have a positive disposition and perspective regarding the thing being sought. We are urged to be positive before, during, and after the prayer request is voiced. James informs us that if we are double-minded, we will not receive anything from the Lord. Positive thinking is a component of faith, not the total embodiment of faith or a synonym for faith.

In his popular book *The Power of Positive Thinking*, Norman Vincent Peale defines positive thinking: "Believe in yourself! Have faith in your abilities! Without a humble but reasonable confidence in your own powers you cannot be successful or happy. But with sound self-confidence you can succeed."[3] In distinguishing between faith and positive thinking, one can readily see that faith includes two parties: God and a human being. On the other hand, positive thinking includes only one party: a person who holds to a confident, self-assured, and independent perspective of himself or herself. Arguably we are called to think positively as Paul exhorted the Philippians—"Whatever is true, whatever is noble, whatever is right . . . think about such things" (4:8)—but within a framework of having faith in and reliance on God. Positive thinking without the underpinnings of biblical faith leads to independence from God, which is the complete antithesis of faith. Faith brings us to God for his help and guidance (Heb. 11:6), while positive thinking alone keeps us away from God.

Quite often people mistake positive thinking for faith. They presume they are applying their faith to a situation, when all along they are merely exhibiting a self-assured position. This self-confident disposition often blinds people from seeing the presumptions that stem from positive thinking. Positive thinking and faith appear quite similar, at least in their number of composite ingredients. Both are comprised of the three variables: knowledge, belief, and assent. A major difference between faith and positive thinking is in the first ingredient, *knowledge*. Someone who mistakes presumptive actions for faith actions often errs in the area of knowledge. The information that provides the basis for a confident assertion is largely erroneous knowledge, bad data, unscriptural assumptions, or limited information.

An example is the single guy who sees a beautiful woman and blurts out to himself, "I claim her for my wife, in Jesus's name!" He has knowledge (albeit faulty), believes the knowledge he has, and begins to assent to the idea. To his dismay, she has no interest in him and marries someone else. In anger he screams out to God in prayer, "I believed you by faith for that woman. Faith does not work!" Where did he go wrong? His error was in his body of knowledge. He presumed that God would serve as his personal bellhop and that the Scriptures gave him the authority to simply claim whatever woman he wanted for marriage. This is simply erroneous. Accurate knowledge of the Bible, along with accurate information about the item or objective being sought and the way in which each bears upon the other, is key to establishing the right foundational ingredient to faith—knowledge.

As the story goes, a positive thinker greeted a co-worker one morning. The co-worker responded in a low, somber tone. "What's wrong, Frank?" the positive thinker asked sympathetically. "My brother is sick," Frank said. At that, the positive thinker, who believed that right thinking could solve all of life's maladies, said, "No! Your brother is not sick. He *thinks* he's sick. It's all in his mind." A week later Frank was looking pretty sad again. "What's wrong?" his co-worker asked. Frank said, "My brother thinks he's dead." Positive thinking and faith are two entirely different things.

If you've been around the church for any time, I'm sure you have heard a lot of fantastic stories about the misuse of faith. These excessive actions carried out by zealous people don't represent the Bible's definition of true faith. Even though many people have innocently misapplied the laws of faith, Scripture reminds us, "Without faith it is impossible to please God" (Heb. 11:6).

To avoid all the nightmares of misguided faith, simply keep these three ingredients in front of you whenever faith is called for: knowledge + belief + assent = faith.

I too made some major mistakes in attempting to exercise faith in the early years of my Christian walk. But now that I've recovered my dignity from most of these spiritual blunders, I am happy to pass on what I've learned to you. Nevertheless, feel free to laugh at my zealousness as you learn about the principles of faith.

Stumbling on Faith

I came to Christ as one who had fancied himself an academic, a scientist, and a skeptic. Though my family attended a church for a couple of years during my pre-teens, religion didn't really take root in my young life. When I think back on our brief church attendance, my lack of commitment to religion is not surprising. To my recollection, the minister's twenty-minute Sunday sermon, though perhaps well intended, had little to do with Jesus, salvation, or the Bible. It never made much of an impression on me. But then again, I wasn't paying much attention to what he said. In fact, I used to fall asleep during the preaching. One annoyed lady telephoned my mother complaining that I was sleeping during the sermon every week. When my mother confronted me, I simply said, "Sunday is the day of rest."

We stopped attending when I was around thirteen, and that was the end of my boyhood religious education. Not long afterward I quit believing altogether and became a teenage atheist. My motto was "Show me God in a test tube and I'll believe."

I went off to college at age sixteen with a personal mission to earn a Ph.D. by the time I reached twenty-five. I really didn't go out of my way to antagonize Christians, but whenever I encountered a person of faith, I would immediately go on the offensive. I had a prideful contempt of all serious religious people (particularly Christians) because I considered them not only intellectually inferior but also intellectually dishonest. In my opinion, they had turned off their minds, rejected reason, and ignored proven scientific facts in order to embrace things by faith alone. That disgusted and infuriated me.

Even though I was outwardly skeptical about any kind of spiritual reality, about midway through my undergraduate years, I began to consider the most radical of all ideas—the existence of some kind of god. This was so contrary to my previous philosophy and life perspective that even entertaining the possibility was disturbing. I had thoroughly programmed my mind in a way that left no room for thoughts about God, and I reinforced this programming by my atheistic values and the friends I hung around with.

When I embraced Christ as Savior, this event marked the culmination of a yearlong process of introspection. I began contemplating my future life—my early adulthood through middle adult years that lay ahead—and concluded that there must be more to life than getting a good job, a great wife, and a lot of money, though I had none of those things yet. My sarcastic, secular friends also helped me make a decision for Christ. I became tired of the emptiness of life—at least the way they portrayed it—and began to crave something else. Something more valuable and long lasting became my focus, but I did not know what it was, or how or where to find what I was looking for.

Imagine how surprised everyone was when I wholeheartedly accepted Jesus Christ as my Savior and immediately began to share my faith. My friends thought I was joking. Christians on campus thought it was a trick. The first time I went to church, the students in the congregation were

24

sure I had followed them to the worship service to publicly antagonize them. They could scarcely believe I had actually become a Christian.

Paul wrote to the Romans about renewing their minds with the Word of God (Rom. 12:2). I had a lot of mental reprogramming to do. Using the same fervor with which I had questioned the validity of faith as a skeptic, I began to search the Scriptures as a new believer, seeking answers about the nature and the dynamics of the Christian faith. Today I am an ordained minister, a seminary graduate with an earned Ph.D., and the pastor of a congregation of five thousand parishioners of twenty-five different nationalities.

Over the last two decades of walking with Jesus, I have studied people and how they deal with life. And in my pastoral role, I have the opportunity to see people at the high points of their lives and others at their lowest moments. It may be the birth of a long-awaited baby or the untimely death of a loved one. One common denominator evident in all of these experiences is the need for faith to be applied in real-life situations.

Some people constantly struggle emotionally, materially, or spiritually, because either they don't know or have not heeded the biblical command "Have faith in God" (Mark 11:22). When Jesus uttered the words "Have faith," they were spoken in the active imperative voice. This grammatical tense conveys a command spoken in the present, interpreted as an ongoing occurrence. In other words, Jesus's audience understood his command (Have faith in God!) to mean that they were to have faith and *always continue* to have faith in God.

The foundational key to exercising faith is that you must become a member of *the* Christian faith. My personal quest to know God through faith, which began back in college, became a lifelong journey on a road that quickly became rough and steep. That upward journey of faith is what this book is all about.

Saving Faith

My coming to believe in the God of the Bible and accepting the salvation he provides through Jesus Christ, his only Son, was a great step forward but still merely an intellectual assent to a belief *about* God. Soon I took another big leap—believing that God actually loves *me* and that Christ died for *my sins*. I did not come to understand these issues on my own; no one does. The Holy Spirit had begun to convict me both of his presence and of my sin.

With the knowledge of God's Word and the urging of the Spirit, I discovered a deal I could not turn down—my sin in exchange for his salvation. At that point my belief was transformed into something very different. It was no longer merely a belief about God but a faith that appropriated the promise of God experientially. It was "saving faith," as many have called it.

Living Faith

For any new Christian, there is plenty to celebrate by coming to this "saving faith." If your primary objective is simply to get to heaven, there is hardly a compelling reason to press on. However, God's plan and purpose do not end there. There are higher levels and lessons about faith yet to come. Saving faith grows into a *living faith* in which you learn to trust God always and in every circumstance.

People who have been consistently growing in faith for many years have a quiet confidence that is unshakable in the face of any obstacle, opposition, or delay. With regard to the promises of God in their lives, it is more than just believing, hoping, and trusting; it is an inner knowing. This is what the writer of Hebrews referred to when he said, "Faith is the assurance of things hoped for, the conviction of things not seen" (11:1 NASB).

Let me illustrate this type of faith. During my former days as an atheist, I was bewildered at how people could believe there was a God. What was so hard for me seemed so easy for them. After I began to believe in God, I was amazed at how Christians could be so sure that God loved them and that they were actually saved. Again, it was easy for them but hard for me. But after I received Christ into my life, I found that I too had that same confidence. By that time an intellectual belief in God was no longer an issue for me. And I no longer had any doubts about my salvation. I had the full assurance that I was cleansed by Christ's blood, that I was completely forgiven, and that the Holy Spirit lived within me.

Similarly, as new believers grow in faith, the things they struggled to believe at one level become a matter of inner confidence and assurance on the next. God's plan and purpose for each of us is that we develop living faith and grow it to the degree that it bridges the gap between the spiritual and the physical worlds.

Throughout my years as a pastor, I have seen this kind of quiet assurance in a lot of people. For these "seasoned saints," as I call them, deep, abiding, fully assured faith doesn't seem to be a struggle. One who comes to mind is Ann Brown, a remarkable woman who is often called into action by some desperate person seeking peace, advice, or comfort. Throughout almost thirty years of carrying her cross, fighting the devil, and overcoming unusual trials, Ann has developed the ability to maintain her composure without breaking a sweat. This inner resolve in God's amazing grace is almost palpable as she challenges younger believers to trust in God's love during trying times.

The conviction of things not seen is as natural and easy for these seasoned saints as seeing the tangible world is for the rest of us. In terms of spirituality, these saints fit into an elite category in my estimation. And you don't just arrive there without a process.

Some Inductees in the Hall of Faith

The eleventh chapter of Hebrews is commonly referred to as "the Hall of Faith." This term is a takeoff from the phrase *Hall of Fame*, an esteemed society of record-breaking professional athletes who have retired from their sport. The parallel was drawn to highlight the Hebraic writer's assemblage of seventeen men and women who through faith in God obtained significant promises for their lives and generation. The Bible holds up this specific list of characters plus others

28

not mentioned by name as stellar examples of faith heroes. All of their stories speak of the day (or mental perspective) before the miracles began.

Starting with Abel, the Bible cites that the day before his act of faith he had an honoring perspective of God. In the case of Enoch, the day before the miracle it was said that he "pleased God" (Heb. 11:5). With Noah, his obedience to God's warnings prefaced God's miracles. In Abraham's account, the writer tells us he obeyed God (Heb. 11:8). In the case of the prostitute Rahab, she welcomed the Hebrew spies without disclosing their clandestine activities. All of these faith heroes had the right mind-set concerning faith *before* the miracles began. From these godly examples, we can conclude that if you adopt the right understanding of faith, coupled with right actions, miracles are certain to flow. Expect God to answer your prayers asked in faith!

two

KNOWING WHEN TO QUIT
(*Never!*)

The lessons of faith don't necessarily wait for you to become a strong Christian. One of the most difficult battles of faith I ever encountered began almost immediately after I came to Christ.

All my life I wanted to become an engineer. My two brothers and I devoured every copy of *Popular Mechanics* magazine Dad brought home. As soon as we were old enough to work a screwdriver, we began taking apart everything in the house to see if we could put it back together and make it work again. At age sixteen, I entered Fairleigh Dickinson University (in New Jersey) on a partial athletic scholarship. Throughout my college years, I had been a skeptic and a persecutor of Christians. Two months after graduating with a bachelor's degree in mechanical engineering, I gave my life to Jesus Christ.

In the fall of that same year, I began a master's program in civil engineering at Stevens Institute of Technology (also in New Jersey). Moved by the joy of my newfound faith, I immediately became an evangelist on campus and a man of faith and prayer. Six months before graduation, one of my foremost prayers was that God would help me find just the right job as a civil engineer upon graduation.

Armed with a grade point average of 3.6 and the prestige of a full academic scholarship, in the back of my mind I felt that landing a job was a done deal, especially since I had been praying about this and other topics for quite some time. I expected to have my pick. A month or two went by. Though I had been invited to an impressive number of interviews, I had not received a single offer. Beginning to feel the pressure, I boldly said, "Lord, if you will give me a job in my field, I'll give you a tithe (10 percent) of everything I earn!" Three months before graduation—still no job.

I decided to sweeten the offer, upping the ante to 15 percent. I know now that it's useless and doctrinally incorrect to attempt to bribe God. I was, however, a young Christian, and the proposal made perfect sense to me then. By the time graduation day came, the ante was up to 20 percent; still no job in my field.

Shortly after graduation, I finally landed a job. I didn't begin as an engineer, designing power plants or sophisticated environmental systems. Rather, my job was in a spaghetti factory, standing on a thirty-foot platform dropping spaghetti down a chute eight hours a day. It was the only job I could find. Every other door I knocked on was slammed in my face.

I sent out résumés to hundreds of companies from New Jersey to Saudi Arabia. Yet every company I applied to turned me down. At the same time, my classmates were stepping into great engineering jobs, despite their having little or no faith, less experience, and lower GPAs than me. It was as though God himself were resisting me at every turn. I reasoned that God was trying to teach me something—even though I used every trick I knew to get out of his classroom. One of the lessons I simply couldn't escape was that once God gets you in his vise grips, there's no use in struggling to get out.

James writes in his letter, "Consider it pure joy, my brothers, whenever you face trials of many kinds, because you know that the testing of your faith develops perseverance. Perseverance must finish its work so that you may be mature and complete, not lacking anything" (1:2–4). Consider it all joy? You've got to be kidding! I sure didn't feel much joy at the time. J. B. Phillips, the New Testament Greek scholar, translates verses 2 and 3 this way: "When all kinds of trials and temptations crowd into your lives, my brothers, don't resent them as intruders, but welcome them as friends!" Imagine sitting in your living room and the doorbell rings. You look out the peephole, and it's the embodiment of a big ol' nasty trial.

"Well, come on in!" you say. "Good to see you again. It's been far too long."

Now, I'm not suggesting—nor does the Bible imply—that you become some weirdo who actively invites trials to your doorstep. But you do need to endure them with patience when they arrive. James tells us to welcome them with a joyful attitude, because God is using them to grow our faith.

Eventually I quit being a spaghetti factory worker to take a better-paying job. At that point, the only job I could find was at Clairol—not in the corporate offices, but in a factory, sorting bottles of hair spray into boxes and then dumping the boxes into labeling chutes. By this time, I was alternating emotionally between bold confessions of faith for the "real" job that I longed for and the depths of despair because of the real job that I had.

One day on my lunch break at the Clairol factory, my emotions came to a head. I went out to sit in my old beat-up jalopy. Everything was wrong with that car. It barely ran, and when it did, the chassis shook and squeaked so annoyingly that people would stop and look as I drove by. Sitting in that car was depressing enough, but what added to my despair was that I didn't have any food at home to make lunch and I didn't have any money to buy lunch. I pulled out my pocket New Testament and began to read. The more I read, the angrier I became. I said out loud, "Look at what God says about himself in his Word. And look at the job I am doing." Then I began to pray. Actually, I was arguing with God. I remember as clearly as if it were yesterday. I yelled, "God, this is not right!" with tears rolling down my cheeks, anger welling up in my heart, and disappointment filling my mind. I was screaming at the top of my lungs as I sat in the parking lot with the windows rolled up. People must have thought I had gone over the edge. They were probably right.

That day, for one of the first times in my life, the Holy Spirit spoke to me with crystal clarity. "David," he said, "if I call you to work in this job for the rest of your life, will you do it?"

I answered the Holy Spirit, "Yes, if that is your plan for me, that is what I will do."

There was a real breakthrough in my life that day. In the short time I had been a Christian, I had considered a job in civil engineering to be God's promise and the answer to my prayers. That day in the car, I didn't know if I would ever work a day in my life as an engineer. And though I didn't know what God was calling me to do, and I didn't get the job I had hoped for that day, I received something even better—an unexplainable assurance of things hoped for and a rock-solid conviction of things not seen. Whatever God had in mind for me, he would bring it to pass—no doubt about it. How did I know that? Well, I can't say exactly, but I knew that I knew that I knew that what God had promised, he would bring to pass. He promised his guidance and comfort throughout my disorientation with my search for a job in the field of engineering. And I made a commitment to stand in faith to await the promise.

Sometimes we become angry and frustrated with God because things do not work out the way we think they should or as quickly as we would like. I had my one-year, three-year, and five-year plans, but God scrubbed my plans so he could work in me something he wanted. The experience burned a lot of the pride out of my life. And although I didn't realize it back then, God was preparing me to serve others.

I eventually practiced civil engineering in the consulting engineering field for seven years, until God revealed the next step in his promise and calling for me. But during my tenure in engineering, I held my career loosely and with more humility than I would have if God hadn't taken me through that earlier process. I learned to want his promise, not my plan.

I took four unforgettable lessons away from this experience:

1. The power of faith is not solely for appropriating God's promises or for getting our needs met, but to preserve our personal values, morals, and ethics.
2. Full assurance of faith is a combination of our decision to stand in faith and the Holy Spirit working in our lives, giving us the grace to believe.
3. God gives us grace to become fully assured about his promises and his plan, not necessarily our plans and our desires.
4. Being fully assured about God's faithfulness to bring about his promises and his plan in our lives does not come to the casual seeker.

The Power of Persistence

It takes persistence and perseverance to inherit the promises of God birthed through faith. If one door closes, you have to knock on the next one and the next and the next and the next.

Yet that goes completely against what I often hear people say about faith. They are convinced that if you really, really have faith, you should pray about something only once and never bring it up again. I understand the point they are trying to make—that God hears our prayers and is not forgetful. By this logic there would never be reason to pray at all, because, to be theologically precise, he knows our needs and our prayers before they even enter our mind. When you repeatedly pray about something, it doesn't necessarily mean you do not have faith. You need to keep bringing your requests to God as long as those unfulfilled requests are heavy upon your heart.

When do you stop praying and start thanking? Well, you can and should thank him all along the way. But prayer is a persistent activity that you pursue until you see the answer with your natural eyes or until you are granted "the assurance of things hoped for, the conviction of things not seen" in your heart.

The idea of praying about a matter only once as an expression of great faith is really not in accordance with Christ's practice or teaching. For example, the Scriptures point out that in the Garden of Gethsemane, "Once more he [Jesus] went away and prayed the same thing" (Mark 14:39). This indicates that Jesus repeated his prayer request because his heart was consumed with the matter at hand. Paul admits praying *three* separate times about a thorn in the flesh (2 Cor. 12:8–9). Scholars debate whether this "thorn in the flesh" was an illness or a demonic spirit, but no one disputes the fact that the apostle prayed three times about the same matter. The New Living Translation uses the word *begged* to describe how Paul prayed, which suggests that he was emotionally distressed over the problem.

Similarly, when you are distraught, overly concerned, or mentally charged with a matter, you can repeat the request in prayer in a faith manner to God. Jesus talked about how to knock on a door if you really want it to open. The Williams translation reflects the literal rendering of the Greek aorist tense. "Keep on asking, and the gift will be given you; keep on seeking, and you will find; keep on knocking, and the door will open to you. For everyone who keeps on asking receives, and everyone who keeps on seeking, finds, and to the one who keeps on knocking, the door will be open" (Matt. 7:7–8, Williams).

Real biblical faith is a persistent faith. This is why Jesus told his disciples to keep on asking and the gift would be given. This is not simply repetitive babbling. Our asking should be with wisdom and courage. This is why the words *seeking* and *knocking* are also included with this example of persistence. Persistent prayer demonstrates faith.

Benefits of Perseverance

While it is true that perseverance shows that you have faith, it does not ward off further difficulties or obstacles to your faith. However, a by-product of using faith is that you can develop the character of Christ during trying times. Still, the outcome depends on your response to the crisis.

Some people become bitter, cynical, and uncaring after a difficult trial. As a result, such people have become thieves, terrorists, and atheists. Others allow the trial to produce in them a supernatural compassion for people. For those who persevere in this fight of faith, here are a few of the benefits.

38

1. Perseverance Reinforces Values

The exercise of faith is not solely to help you appropriate God's promises or have your needs met. Following my trials at the spaghetti factory and at the other menial jobs I had to accept during that time, I discovered that walking in faith also allowed me to appropriate the grace of God needed to reinforce and preserve my morals, values, and integrity. Rarely do we hear of this dimension of faith. Yet the Scriptures declare it loud and clear.

> Women received back their dead, raised to life again. Others were tortured and refused to be released, so that they might gain a better resurrection. Some faced jeers and flogging, while still others were chained and put in prison. They were stoned; they were sawed in two; they were put to death by the sword. They went about in sheepskins and goatskins, destitute, persecuted and mistreated—the world was not worthy of them. They wandered in deserts and mountains, and in caves and holes in the ground.
>
> These were all commended for their faith, yet none of them received what had been promised.
>
> Hebrews 11:35–39

This passage in Hebrews references both sides of faith: the one where powerful promises are obtained and the other where integrity is preserved while the promises are still pursued. Who would have thought that being tortured in lieu of compromising your position to gain freedom would be labeled an action of faith? Yet verse 39 calls it "faith."

If I were in a trial for my life as verses 35–39 describe, certainly I would not have chosen to be tortured, jeered, flogged, or chained. I would have told my torturers whatever they wanted to hear, rationalizing the wisdom and prudence of my actions. Yet these brave saints used faith to maintain their commitment and integrity though not every aspect of God's promises was received.

If you currently face a gloomy situation, use your faith to preserve your integrity and righteous values. Don't give in to the temptation of compromise under any circumstance. Trust God to preserve your values while you are waiting for the other dimension of faith to become manifested in your life.

2. Perseverance Is a Preparation for Blessings

Being persistent in your faith is not a ploy to force God to deal with you justly and compassionately, and it's not because God wants to see people beg. Neither is he waiting for us to bribe him with a promise in order to increase our financial giving. The point of Jesus's parable of the unjust judge is that the Father is *not* like that. When you persevere through trial and what seems to be delay, God is working in you to prepare you for his blessings. To put it another way, God is getting you ready for what he's already gotten ready for you. Persistence is not for God but for you.

When I was working at all those minimum-wage jobs and struggling desperately with my faith, God was preparing me. All I could think about was landing a job in civil engineering, but God knew that engineering would be only a temporary career. He was preparing me to serve him as a pastor who knew firsthand the joy of obedience. This trait is learned only in the school of trials. I learned how to enjoy God's will and direction despite the fact that I was doing something I did not want to do. Obedience is about honoring someone else's desire, will, and interests. The joy of obedience is when you obey with a right attitude, disposition, and joyous countenance knowing that God has your best interest at heart.

Before I got caught up in my dream of becoming a brilliant, affluent, and esteemed engineer, God wanted me to know that I was no better than anyone else—no matter what type of work a person does. Only God knew how important it was for me to understand that from the beginning.

If you could move ahead with God's plan for your life on your own timetable, your own unsanctified pride, egotism, and self-will would perhaps become your greatest stumbling block.

Through the process of faith God will do his work in your life so that when he opens the doors to his plan and purpose for you, you are ready to step into whatever that might be.

Why is it so hard to inherit the promises or to find God's plan and purpose? Why does it require such persistence? Because God is getting you ready for what he's already gotten ready for you.

3. Perseverance Causes You to Become an Anchor of Faith

I like hanging around seasoned people. By "seasoned," I don't mean that they are old chronologically, but that they

41

have gone through many crises and persevered in their faith. Consequently, when they go through new trials, they are not moved. Sure, they are bothered somewhat, but they also have an inner resolve and confidence that inspire me.

While most novices to the walk of faith are screaming at the top of their lungs, "This is not right, God!" seasoned saints display a peace that passes all understanding. Faith seems to come much easier to them despite all the chaos around them. Why? Because they are seasoned in the faith. They have seen God do things in their lives before and they know by Scripture *and* experience that God is the same yesterday, today, and forever.

People don't acquire this kind of assurance by having everything go smoothly in their lives. Sure, I've known people who were bold in their faith because the few difficulties they had faced in life had worked out quickly and easily. I am really happy that they have been so fortunate and that things have gone so well for them. But I also know that when they face huge obstacles that appear immovable, they will need encouragement and support from those who have learned some secrets about trusting God through hard times.

There is a big difference between someone who theorizes about faith and the promises of God versus someone who has been through the fire with God. These seasoned veterans of faith are like anchors in the body of Christ. I pray that you would become one of those people—a source of resolve and assurance—and that whatever difficulties come along, you can be an anchor of hope to those facing the storms that you have already come through.

As experiences come your way—all kinds of trials and testing—learning how to persevere anchors and matures you in your walk with the Lord. While you are waiting for the answers to your prayers, God is causing the immature traits of impatience, unrealistic expectations, selfish ambitions, and patterns of an undisciplined lifestyle to melt away. The end result of perseverance is the anchoring of faith and the maturing of character.

Hang On to Confidence

What has God called you to do? What has he spoken to your heart concerning your family, marriage, business, job, kids, ministry, education, or health? Whether it is a promise in the Scripture that you want to appropriate in your life or an inner sense of God's calling, don't expect it to drop out of the sky without a measure of faithfulness and persistence on your part—sometimes a great measure. God uses the vehicle of faith for us to appropriate his promises in our life. He also uses the instrument of faith to bring us into a place of spiritual maturity.

The biblical admonition is "Do not throw away your confidence; it will be richly rewarded. You need to persevere so that when you have done the will of God, you will receive what he has promised" (Heb. 10:35–36). The passage reminds me to hang on to the confidence of things unseen. It also suggests that I can throw it away if I choose. I want to make sure that to the best of my knowledge the various areas of my life are in alignment with the will of God. After I have been diligent to knock on all the doors, sought God's guidance, persistently asked, gone to mentors for counsel, asked God to search my heart—after I have done the will of God—I will stand in faith with confidence and persistence so that in time I too will receive what was promised.

Picture this: A friend was flying from San Francisco to Los Angeles. The plane unexpectedly stopped in Sacramento on the way. The flight attendant explained that there would be a delay, and if passengers wanted to get off the aircraft, they would reboard in thirty minutes. Everybody got off the plane except one gentleman who was blind. My friend noticed him as he walked by, and could tell he had flown before because his seeing-eye dog lay quietly underneath the seats in front of him throughout the entire flight. He could also tell the man had flown this same flight before because the pilot approached him and called him by name, saying, "Keith, we're in Sacramento for almost an hour. Would you like to get off and stretch your legs?"

Keith replied, "No thanks, but maybe my dog would like to stretch his legs."

Imagine this: All the people in the gate area came to a complete standstill when they saw the pilot walk off the plane with the seeing-eye dog! The pilot was even wearing sunglasses. People scattered. They not only tried to change planes but also tried to change airlines. They had lost their confidence.

The lesson in this story: Don't lose confidence and change your plans midstream because things aren't what they appear to be. Trust God's leadership to bring his promise to fruition through your use of faith.

three

___

THE JOURNEY OF FAITH
DEFINED

As a new believer, I began to seek answers about the definition and dynamics of faith. With the same fervor with which I had questioned the validity of faith as a skeptic, I wanted to understand what it meant to have faith. I was a year away from completing a master's degree in civil engineering, and of course, we engineers have to be precise about everything.

"Define what you mean by faith," I would ask Christians, as if they could simply look up the specs in a technical manual. The most common reply was something like, "Well, it's just believing God." That did not at all satisfy me.

45

"And what does it really mean to believe God?" I pressed. "To have faith, of course," my friends would respond.

After several conversations like this, I thought to myself, *We seem to be stuck in a circle of semantics and going nowhere.* I felt like Spurgeon when he queried a man about his beliefs. The man said, "I believe what my church believes." At that Spurgeon asked, "And what does your church believe?" "My church believes what I believe," replied the man. With a tone of irritation, Spurgeon followed up, "What do you and your church believe?" "We believe the same thing," the man replied. Like Spurgeon, I eventually gave up the questions, but certainly not the quest.

Now I realize that defining faith is not an easy task. It's like trying to explain terms like *being, reality, eternity,* or *time.* These concepts are so closely integrated in our everyday lives, it is difficult to articulate how they are applied to our lives, much less their meaning. Similarly, the practical applications and outworkings of faith are complex and take a lifetime to learn.

Yet I'd like to begin by defining faith as *inheriting the covenant promises of God.*

The Underpinnings of New Testament Faith

The idea of inheriting the covenant promises of God by faith is rooted in Old Testament history and theology. Therefore, it is important that we examine the covenant, or agreement, God established with Abraham, the father of faith.

First we must discover what the covenant is about. What promises were made by the covenant? What were the conditions of the covenant? Who are the heirs of that covenant? Here are some of the fundamental points about both the old covenant and the new covenant to serve as a foundation for our building faith that is fully assured:

- God made a covenant with Abram (Abraham's original name) and his descendants. They then became God's covenant people, or chosen people.
- The promise to Abram was that he would become the father of many nations and that to his descendants through Isaac they would be given a land and made into a nation.
- The conditions of these covenant promises to the children of Israel were the requirements of the law.
- The Old Testament prophets promised that a Messiah would come to reestablish the seed of David upon the throne of Israel and establish the kingdom of God. They also foretold of a new covenant that would surpass the old.
- When Jesus the Messiah arrived, he was not what the Jews had expected. He was not a military or political leader. He did not expel the occupying Roman forces. Instead of becoming the king of a restored Israel, he was crucified by the Romans.
- Jesus, personally and through his apostles, radically reinterpreted the meaning of the kingdom and the covenant. The Messiah was to suffer and die as the

47

unblemished sacrificial Lamb of God, taking away the sins of the world. The kingdom of God was not of this world, but a spiritual kingdom. Christ is referred to as the Son of David who is forever seated at the right hand of God (Acts 2:30–33).

- For the descendants of Abraham, Isaac, and Jacob, the gospel was a hard pill to swallow. (1) The "seed of Abraham" (seed can be singular or plural) referred to Christ himself, not the Jews. (2) The heirs of the promise were those who were children of Abraham by faith, not by blood. Even uncircumcised Gentiles by faith in Christ were considered heirs of the covenant, while scribes and Pharisees were not. (3) Finally, righteousness was based on faith in the sacrifice of Christ, not in the law of Moses or the ceremonial sacrifices of animals.

Can you imagine how the Jews must have felt? The temple, the sacrifices, the law, and even their status as biological descendants of Abraham had suddenly (according to Jesus and the apostles) become largely insignificant because a new covenant had superceded the old. It is easy to see why they reacted so violently.

The apostle Paul goes on to explain the place of faith in the new covenant. What he says is essentially this:

- The covenant promise of God was made not to the many biological descendants of Abraham but to the one descendant—Jesus of Nazareth (Gal. 3:16).
- The sacrifice of Christ completely fulfilled all the requirements of the covenant.

48

- By faith we are in Christ and joint heirs with Christ to the promises of God (Rom. 8:16–17).
- Since the promise is by faith, not works of the law, we have a certain assurance. The certainty of the new covenant is expressed in Romans 4:16: "For this reason it is by faith, that it might be in accordance with grace, in order that the promise may be certain to all the descendants, not only to those who are of the Law, but also to those who are of the faith of Abraham, who is the father of us all" (NASB).

How can we have a certain assurance about our salvation and the promises of God? Think about it like this: Outside of Christ, there are no covenant promises. Because we stand in Christ's righteousness by faith, we stand with Christ as coheirs of the promises of God.

Paul wrote to the Corinthians, "For as many as may be the promises of God, in Him they are yes" (2 Cor. 1:20 NASB). Knowing the promises God extends to you is of utmost importance. Imagine living like a pauper when a $100 million inheritance is sitting in the bank designated solely to you. Lack of knowledge about the sum of money keeps you living outside its benefits.

If you are misinformed or unaware of the promises designated for you by God, you are missing the rich quality of life that knowledge of these promises can bring. If you have fallen into this mental and emotional trap of discouragement, may the Holy Spirit use this book to release you to enjoy the destiny God has for you through your actions of faith. As you can see, knowing the promises and applying faith to see them realized are two different things entirely. Both are important, yet separate. The first step of knowing the promises of God for your life occurs when you read the Bible and ask the question, What promise is in this passage for me? The second step of embracing the promises happens when the following biblical principles of faith are implemented.

Practical Dynamics of Faith

As I have said, Hebrews 11 is commonly known as the "Hall of Faith." Here great men and women of the Bible are commended for their faith and held up as examples for others. The writer introduces these great heroes of faith by saying, "Now faith is being sure of what we hope for and certain of what we do not see" (11:1). This definition of faith has many shades of meaning.

1. Faith as a Title Deed

Some biblical scholars have suggested this possible translation of Hebrews 11:1—"Faith is the *title deed* of things we hope for." In this sense, having faith is similar to holding the title deed to a piece of real estate. What if I challenged your right to the parcel of land to which you hold the title deed? What if I claimed it as my own and threatened to remove you forcibly from the premises? You would probably respond to my demands by going through your legal papers, pulling out the title deed, and going before the authorities with confidence because you had irrefutable proof of ownership in your hand.

A friend of mine who is an engineer told me the story of his recent job promotion. He had written a lengthy and technical report that he gave to one of his colleagues to hand in to the supervisor. But his colleague took full credit for the report when he saw how his boss was raving about its brilliance. When my friend chimed in and said he was the one who wrote it, his colleague called him a liar and said that he was the one who really penned the document. At that my friend said, "Let me go home and get all of the handwritten notes and calculations. I always keep the original raw documents at home." Upon hearing this talk of furnishing the "title deed," the colleague spent the remainder of the meeting squirming and chain-smoking because he was about to be discovered.

In a spiritual sense, your faith is proof that you are the owner of and heir to God's promise. F. F. Bruce writes, "It might no doubt be said that if we adopt this meaning here (i.e., faith as the title deed), we have something comparable to Paul's language about the Holy Spirit as the 'first fruits' or 'earnest' (down payment) of the coming inheritance of believers."[1]

Bruce refers to several verses in the New Testament. One of those is Ephesians 1:13–14, which says, "Having believed, you were marked in him with a seal, the promised Holy Spirit, who is a deposit guaranteeing our inheritance until the redemption of those who are God's possession." So we might say that faith is the title deed to an inheritance we have received, and the down payment of that inheritance is the gift of the Holy Spirit sent to live in our hearts.[2]

The title deed to God's promises must be secured through prayer. Rees Howells, the twentieth-century intercessor who helped usher in the Welsh revivals, calls this perspective on faith "the grace of faith."[3] In essence, Howells espouses the view, with which I wholeheartedly concur, that the person who has secured an answer or an internal witness in prayer possesses the authority and an assurance of the thing hoped for. Although not ultimately experienced as it will be in heaven, God's promise and the believer's internal resolve of the receipt of God's will are so certain that we experience grace with all the security of a title deed.

This "title deed praying" has nothing to do with the length of time you pray—whether hours, days, or weeks. Your intense prayer, charged with honesty, candidness, and sincerity concerning the object of your desire, releases the grace of God that grants you the title deed concerning your request.

Prior to entering full-time Christian ministry, I worked as a civil engineer in the environmental consulting field. Simultaneously my wife and I were in our second year of pastoral ministry, caring for the fledgling work we had planted. Although the congregation was no more than forty members, I knew God had called me into full-time pastoral work. Yet the idea of resigning from my lucrative engineering career to pastor Christ Church full-time seemed ridiculous to me. How was the church going to support me when it could barely make ends meet? I had a wife and a newborn baby. It just didn't make sense.

Nevertheless, the thought of serving God full-time would not leave me alone, though I had rationalized it away as unfeasible and nonsensical. I prayed about the matter halfheartedly, but I was more concerned about the finances than I was about hearing God's direction. My faith wavered day after day.

One evening Marlinda and I spoke openly to each other about my desire to enter full-time ministry and about the fear that plagued my mind.

"Honey, I am at peace about your leaving engineering," Marlinda said. "Don't worry. God will provide for our family."

Fueled by Marlinda's words of comfort and reassurance, I entered into passionate prayer that evening, pouring out my feelings of ambivalence and fear to the Lord. I ended by saying to the Lord, "I want your will more than anything else. What do you want me to do?"

In that very prayer session I received the title deed for my faith. The Lord gave me an inward assurance that he would provide for me if I would only trust him. The next day I turned in my resignation letter, indicating that I would work part-time two days a week in engineering and the other three days a week in ministry. My employers agreed to that offer. Remarkably, within six weeks I had to go completely full-time because the church doubled numerically. Fifteen years and five thousand members later, I can look back to that prayer time and say confidently that the destiny of our church was triggered when I received the title deed of my faith for full-time ministry.

2. Faith as Substance

The King James Version uses this language in Hebrews 11:1—"Now faith is the substance of things hoped for." The original Greek term for "substance" here (*hypostasis*) is also used in Hebrews 1:3 to describe Jesus Christ as the *hypostasis* (or "substance" or "exact representation") of God's nature.[4] In both these cases, ownership of what is hoped for is an intangible concept. You can see the *evidence* of ownership, but you can't really see the ownership itself. What you can see and feel is the substance of a title deed. In the same way, faith is the *hypostasis*, the substance, the ground of confidence that underlies the apparent proof or title deed of things hoped for, providing evidence of things not seen.

Faith as *substance* is an oxymoron—like dry water, cold heat, or dark light. To the natural way of thinking, faith is one thing and substance is something entirely different. Believers accept the fact that faith calls them to accept things by faith when there is in fact no substance on which to base their belief. So when it comes to a question of the "reality" of our inheritance, the question becomes, "Is it by faith or is it substance?" From God's point of view the answer is simply "Yes!" The Scripture says faith *is* the substance of what we hope for. And what we hope for are the fulfilled and manifested promises of God's covenant.

A good example of this God kind of faith is found in Paul's letter to the Romans: "As it is written: 'I [God] have made you [Abraham] a father of many nations.' He is our father in the sight of God, in whom he believed—the God who gives life to the dead and calls things that are not as though they were" (Rom. 4:17).

God calls things that are not as though they were. He can do that because he is God. He sees the future, and what he proposes to do is as real as if it were already done. If it sounds strange for us mere humans to speak of things that do not exist as though they were, think of it this way: Faith is simply agreeing with what God says. Consequently, walking by faith means accepting the fact that you have received promises from God even though you have not yet seen them with your natural eyes.

Look at the next verse in Romans 4 to see how Abram responded to God's promise: "Against all hope, Abraham in hope believed and so became the father of many nations, just as it had been said to him, 'So shall your offspring be'" (Rom. 4:18).

When God made his promise to Abram, he also changed Abram's name to Abraham, which means "father of a multitude" or "father of many nations." Imagine all the years Abraham spent growing into an old man with no children. Every time he spoke his own name, he was proclaiming to the hearer, "I am the father of many nations (*by faith*)." Contrary to all reason and expectation, Abraham believed. And it was by that faith that the promise became a visible reality in this world. Isaac was born, and through his descendants came a great nation.

Unfortunately, people occasionally catch on to this idea and wander off into some strange applications of their theology. When asked, "Do you have the money to buy that new car?" they respond, "Yes, I have the money (*by faith*)." Sometimes their assertion of "by faith" is merely *presumption.*

When people depart from faith into presumption, this divergence typically has something to do with presuming about method and timing. Abraham was fully assured in his faith that God had made him the father of many nations.

But he did not know how or when it would happen. When Abraham got tired of waiting, he made a wrong move and took the timing and the method into his own hands. The result was a son born through a concubine. That turned out to be a painful lesson. In the same way, you may indeed have that new car by faith (really presumption), but you also probably do not know the means or the timing. Consequently, when you become impatient and sign the papers by presumption (not truly by faith) at the car dealership, you too might be in for a painful lesson.

3. Faith as Assurance

I like to think of the word *faith* as an acronym—Full Assurance In The Heart. *Hypostasis* in Hebrews 11:1 is most commonly translated "assurance." The New American Standard Bible reads, "Faith is the assurance of things hoped for."

Faith, as the writer of Hebrews describes here, is much more than vague hope. It was not enough to say that faith is merely *elpis*, the noun form of the Greek verb that means "to hope for." It is much more than that. Faith is the *hypostasis* of things *elpizo*—the assurance, the substance, the title deed of things hoped for. Faith is being fully assured in your heart about the things you hope for, the things you desire, the things you long for, the promises God has given you. It is an inner resolve, an assurance, a peaceful tranquility. Faith is an enduring, unwavering confidence that what you have hoped for is no longer future but present.

Notice what Jesus said to his disciples about faith with regard to assurance: "If anyone says to this mountain, 'Go

56

throw yourself into the sea,' and *does not doubt in his heart* . . . whatever you ask for in prayer, believe that you *have received it*, and it will be yours" (Mark 11:23–24, emphasis added). Jesus did not say that you should believe you *will* receive but that you should believe you *have* received. Faith is not future; it is now. That constitutes the difference between hope and the substance of things hoped for.

Faith that becomes substance and is evidence of unseen promises is hard to explain. I often have to rehearse the concepts surrounding faith repeatedly until they become clear to me again. It is the kind of assurance that can be described with the words "I know that I know that I know . . . even though I'm not sure how I know." This kind of faith is supported and energized by the presence of the Holy Spirit in our lives, giving us his peace, which Paul describes as "the peace of God, which transcends all understanding" (Phil. 4:7).

Abraham discovered this level of faith by going through a dark season in his life, when he cried out to God for an assurance of his promise of a son. Let's look at what happened:

> Then the word of the LORD came to him: "This man will not be your heir, but a son coming from your own body will be your heir." He [God] took him outside and said, "Look up at the heavens and count the stars—if indeed you can count them." Then he said to him, "So shall your offspring be."
>
> Abram believed the LORD, and he [God] credited it to him as righteousness.
>
> Genesis 15:4–6

In Abraham's case, the faith assurance from God came when he looked up at the countless number of stars. This illustration of the future became indelibly printed in his memory. It became a constant reminder of God's plan to honor his promise of making Abraham the father of many nations. Whenever Abraham became weary of waiting for the fulfillment of God's promise, all he had to do was walk outside his tent on a nice clear night and view the stars. Gazing at the stars would keep his faith intact.

Assurance can come in many different forms. Regardless of the packaging, God must be the author of the image that brings you confidence. The apostle Paul had a vision while in Troas of a man in Macedonia begging him, "Come over to Macedonia and help us" (Acts 16:9). The vision assured Paul of God's involvement in his risky evangelistic campaigns. The assurance sustained him to maintain his zeal and aggressiveness to witness to and disciple people in awkward places where his life could be jeopardized. Likewise, you must labor in prayer to gain the necessary assurance surrounding your faith. Internal confidence is an unmistakable source of great strength when forging through uncharted waters by faith.

Your striving to gain assurance of faith is part of having an active relationship with God. To pursue God in prayer is to admit that your relationship is a dynamic one—it's alive and requires attention and input. Both Abraham and Paul actively pursued God. Their faith in God reflected their trust in him. It also showed that a relationship with God is vital to the ongoing attainment of his promises.

The flip side of this statement is equally true. The lack of faith is a reflection of a dying or lifeless relationship with God. Only people who are pursuing God apply faith. Neither backsliders nor nonbelievers have any basis for claiming God's promises or advancing toward a destination where the Lord is the primary leader of their lives.

A man called Father Nash was a famed intercessor who labored with the nineteenth-century American revivalist Charles Finney. Father Nash arose out of a backslidden spiritual state to become a powerful man of faith and prayer. His continuous cry in prayer was for Finney's effectiveness in preaching. Concerning Nash, Finney wrote:

> He would pray until he got an assurance in his mind that God would be with me in preaching, and sometimes he would pray himself ill. I have known the time when he has been in darkness for a season, while the people were gathering, and his mind was full of anxiety, and he would go again and again to pray, till finally he would come into the room with a placid face, and say: "The Lord has come, and He will be with us."[5]

Father Nash would travel to the towns weeks prior to Finney's meetings and intercede for the souls of lost people in that town. Often he would spend days in complete fasting and intercession until he secured by faith the title deed or assurance for the salvation of hundreds of residents of that community. At times he would establish a list of the "rankest" sinners of the town and pray specifically for their conversion.

Most people, especially Christians, have heard of the famed evangelist Charles G. Finney, but few have heard of the humble intercessor Father Nash. The latter changed the world by securing, through faith, the title deed for the souls of multiple thousands. This occurred because his backslidden heart was rekindled into a burning flame for Jesus Christ.

If you want to secure your destiny and obtain the promises of God through faith, make sure your heart is on fire for the Lord. Before you read the next chapter, take a moment to ask yourself this question: Is my heart cold or hot for the Lord? If it is cold or lukewarm, stop right now and turn the place where you are into an altar. Repent of any unconfessed sins and invite the Lord to ignite your heart with his touch. Afterward, read on and learn more about how to "walk on water"—seeing the purposes of God manifested in the lives you touch.

four

~~~~~~~~~~

CULTIVATING AUTHENTIC FAITH

lthough a smattering of Christians have an imbalanced understanding of faith, authentic faith that is powerful and adventurous still exists. Cultivating such a tangible faith requires seeing your trials and predicaments as faith-building opportunities in disguise.

Paul was being transported to Rome to stand trial before Caesar when his ship encountered a terrible storm. After fighting the wind and waves for many days, the ship struck a reef off the coast of Malta and sank. The survivors were able to make it ashore, where the natives of the island showed them great kindness and built a fire for the cold, wet sailors, prisoners, and soldiers.

As Paul was gathering wood for the fire, a snake sprang from the sticks, bit his hand, and hung on. The natives said among themselves, "Undoubtedly this man is a murderer, and though he has been saved from the sea, justice has not allowed him to live" (Acts 28:4 NASB). Malta is home to hundreds of species of snakes, most of which are harmless. The Bible refers to this particular kind of snake as a *viper*, which is quite poisonous. Their venom destroys blood corpuscles and vessels. But Paul simply shook the snake off his hand into the fire and was unharmed. The men of Malta stood there waiting for Paul to swell up, go into convulsions, and die. But having watched him carefully for a long time, they finally changed their minds and began to proclaim excitedly, "He is a god!"

People who are really hungry to grow in faith and walk closer to the Lord have to be careful to avoid the temptation to overspiritualize things. To the men of Malta the snakebite was a sign that Paul was either a murderer or a god—one extreme or the other. However, neither was true. It was a miracle of the Holy Spirit evidenced in Paul's body.

Have you ever been around believers who thought there was a demon or an angel behind every circumstance of life? A lost car key was an attack of the devil, and a traffic light that stayed green just long enough was a miracle of God. At first you may have been impressed or even intimidated by their spirituality, but eventually you realized that their worldview is not quite biblical. I call this unbiblical faith *mystical faith*, which is completely contrary to *authentic faith*.

I recognize that some dimensions of authentic faith are quite mysterious, but not mystical or excessive. In Old Testament days, Moses parted the Red Sea by faith (Exod. 14:16); Elijah was physically translated to heaven by faith (2 Kings 2:11); Elisha caused the ax head to float to the water's surface by faith (2 Kings 6:1–6); and Jeremiah in faith obeyed God's word and prophesied to King Zedekiah while wearing a yoke around his neck (Jer. 28:10). Every one of these deeds was mysterious then and now, yet they all represent authentic faith because they were performed in response to God's spoken word.

On the other hand, mystical faith represents a hyperspiritual perspective that tends to spill over into our ideas about faith and Christian growth, making the things of God appear almost magical. When the gospel began to spread throughout the pagan gentile world, the apostles encountered not unbelief or atheism but a vast assortment of mystical religions. Most can be classified as gnosticism, from the Greek word meaning "knowledge." Gnostics were masters at being spiritual. They were dualists who considered everything spiritual to be good and everything earthly to be inherently evil. Consequently, the idea of God becoming a man in Christ was completely contrary to all they believed.

Gnostics took a similar approach to spiritual maturity. Instead of a realistic, practical application of faith, spiritual advancement was a mystical endowment that dropped down out of heaven on a special chosen few. That kind of mysticism was the background for many of Paul's letters to the churches in Asia Minor.

Avoiding Mystical Faith

To avoid the debilitating traps of mystical faith, try the following five-point acid test to ensure that your faith is authentic.

1. Honor the Bible

Mystical faith tends to ignore the hard, fast rules, doctrines, and guidelines outlined in sacred Scripture, under the pretense that there are exceptions. God's Word declares:

> I warn everyone who hears the words of the prophecy of this book: If anyone adds anything to them, God will add to him the plagues described in this book. And if anyone takes words away from this book of prophecy, God will take away from him his share in the tree of life and in the holy city, which are described in this book.
>
> Revelation 22:18–19

Although this passage's primary reference is to the plagues to be released in the last days, its warning not to blur the jurisdictional authority and boundaries of God's holy Word is clear.

The Bible has been established as a guideline for our benefit. Its intent is not to cordon off joy or fun from our lives. Rather, God is so concerned about our welfare that in his infinite wisdom he tells us, "All Scripture is God-breathed and is useful for teaching, rebuking, correcting and training in righteousness, so that the man of God may be thoroughly equipped for every good work" (2 Tim. 3:16–17). The Bible

64

equips us for every good work, including the parameters in which faith can be employed. All the promises of God—every good work—can be achieved by adhering to the boundaries of the biblical limits.

2. Honor the Biblical Pattern of Faith

Mystical faith seeks a unique pattern, a contemporary unorthodox approach to faith. When you read of the great, spectacular, and fascinating accomplishments that biblical characters were able to achieve through ordinary faith, why try to reinvent the pattern of faith? The Scripture says, "We do not want you to become lazy, but to imitate those who through faith and patience inherit what has been promised" (Heb. 6:12). This passage provides us with insight as to why some people create novel, unsupportable approaches to faith—it is because they are lazy or unwilling to invest the time required to search out the Bible's pattern of faith. A pattern is simply an approach or method used by another that has been sanctioned by God and that works. We are urged to imitate the faith of our spiritual predecessors in our quest to apprehend the things God has promised us.

3. Honor the Safety of Being Scrutinized

No one likes to be scrutinized, critiqued, or inspected—especially when it creates a sense of vulnerability. I realize that the passion to embrace a promise is quite personal and subjective. However, we are not called by God to walk alone without the input of the rest of the body of Christ. The Christian experience automatically engrafts you into a community—a place of belonging and realism where you learn to live with others who share the common experience of salvation through Christ's death and resurrection. This community is built on love—God's love. This unselfish love behooves us to care for the physical, emotional, and spiritual welfare of our spiritual brothers and sisters even to the point of confronting one another lovingly when things appear wrong.

Mystical faith tends to isolate you from the people who love and care for you. This aberrant view of faith creates the internal feeling and idea that no one else understands or values you and your views. Or that no one else is on your plane of faith. They are too carnal, too unspiritual, or too weak in their faith. Thus, you unconsciously or consciously isolate yourself from the people who are trying to hold you accountable for your actions or choices.

About ten years ago I buried a dear woman, a member of my congregation who died an untimely death. She passed away because of her unwillingness to heed my counsel and that of others regarding her stance on faith. She was ill, and rather than taking the medicine that could easily treat her condition, she chose to hold to a mystical faith, claiming that we did not understand that level of faith. I tried to reason with her through the Scriptures, but to no avail.

To avoid this woman's pitfall, maintain a vulnerability regarding your spiritual practices, especially to people who are more experienced than you in the Lord. It will save you from horrible mistakes and unnecessary hardships. Consider all their questions about the object of your faith, the Scriptures you are using as the basis of faith, and the motives behind your desires for the promises you seek. This kind of scrutiny will prove highly beneficial.

4. Honor the Ethical Side of Biblical Faith

In response to Hebrews 10:38—"My righteous one will live by faith"—Origen, one of the church fathers, said, "Faith carries both an ethical and intellectual meaning." He recognized that authentic faith must adhere to Christian ethics.

Ethics involves character, integrity, and values that harmonize with the righteous behavior the Bible calls Christians to practice and support. Mystical faith is consumed with results, namely the attaining of one's desires or needs. This zealousness often can reduce ethics to subservience under the faulty thinking that it is unimportant in light of the faith goal. This is far from the truth.

To understand the importance of ethics and values over selfish actions, one must respect and address the question Francis Schaeffer raised:

> Without some ultimate meaning for a person (for me, an individual), what is the use of living and what will be the basis for morals, values, and law? If one starts from individual acts rather than with an absolute, what gives any real certainty concerning what is right and what is wrong about an individual action?[1]

Schaeffer argues from a questioning perspective that the tenets of the Bible are the absolutes upon which an individual's values should be built.

For example, a husband who is simply weary of tensions in his marriage may suddenly feel "called" to divorce his wife by faith and marry another because they would be "more compatible spiritually." Obviously this "faith statement" too easily ignores the ethical values of a God who hates divorce (see Mal. 2:16). In such a case, the absolutes outlined in the Scriptures should be the basis of the husband's values and actions toward his wife.

As Christians, we cannot compromise our integrity or adherence to biblical values in pursuit of faith goals. When we do, we inadvertently cheapen the quality of faith, reducing it to a mystical nature. To aid us in upholding the Bible's standard on values and ethics, our conscience should always be kept clear and tuned to the convictions of the Holy Spirit.

Authentic faith grows over time through the foundations laid by your prior successful faith ventures (2 Thess. 1:3). If the track record is not there, don't feel obligated or pressured to take on a task outside of your faith parameters. Growth takes time, and God does not push his children through pressure. He gently leads us by his love because he is the Good Shepherd who knows the frailty and health of his sheep.

5. Respect the Test of Faith

Ronald Nash, a professor of philosophy and theology, developed a three-pronged approach to evaluate the plausibility of worldviews—how people see and interpret the world around them.[2] This method of investigation can also be used to determine the likelihood of faith endeavors being categorized as mystical faith or authentic faith. Authentic faith can hold up to this level of scrutiny, unlike mystical faith. The three-pronged approach includes (1) the test of reason, (2) the test of experience, and (3) the test of practice.

The test of reason is the acknowledgment of the veracity of the law of noncontradiction, which postulates that A, which can be anything whatever, cannot be both B and non-B at the same time in the same sense. In other words, if you are able to establish that an orange lies in a category that is distinct, you cannot say that an orange is an apple or a non-orange. This argument would fail the law of non-contradiction.

The test of reason would refute mystical faith if you claimed that God answered your prayers for a Mercedes Benz and the only car you had in your garage was a Toyota Corolla. A Mercedes and a Toyota are two different types of cars. Thus, your faith claim would fail the test of reason because it is contradictory to the facts.

The test of experience is when a faith claim is in harmony with what humanity knows to be true of the physical universe. For example, if one believes in the inherent goodness of people, the realistic observances of the propensity for people to sin would be the test of experience.

Last, the test of practice begs the question: Can the person professing a particular claim of faith live consistently in harmony with the system he or she professes? The test of practice calls for homogeneity in belief, values, and lifestyle practices. Thus, a faith claim that says, "I am believing God that my husband never sins again," does not pass the test of practice. From our lives (or practice), we have learned that every human being sins, even those who sin unconsciously or unintentionally. This faith claim would not be considered an exercise in authentic faith.

As a scientist I am acutely aware of the roles of reason and logic as they relate to supporting one's theories, views, and assumptions. While the notion of faith coupled with reason seems to fall into the category of an oxymoron, it still does not invalidate their union. Faith is not simplemindedness or an uncritical belief—rather, it is an assent to intellect. Clement of Alexandria (ca. AD 215), one of the leading thinkers among the church fathers, wrote, "Faith is intellectual assent to theological propositions because intellect is a gift of God and faith too is a gift of God" (cf. Eph. 2:8).

Conversely, reason has to do with reality and its ability to stand up to scrutiny. The $64,000 question is: Can one be a Bible-believing Christian and a rational thinker at the same time? I believe the two perspectives can and should be integrated to form authentic faith—faith that is plausible, definable, and defendable by the strength of the Bible. Christian educator W. Bingham Hunter shares this same view when he notes, "Faith . . . is a rational response to the evidence of God's self-revelation in nature, human history, the Scriptures and his resurrected Son."[3]

Mystical faith, on the other hand, is not reasonable or plausible to the majority of the Christian community, much less to unbelievers. In other words, mystical faith has no grounds or systematic rationale; it is belief without reason.

I am not lobbying for non-Christians to agree with my desire to use faith or to get their approval as to whether or not a situation calls for faith. What I am striving to show is that whoever queries me about my faith action should be able to hear a plausible, rational, and biblically defensible argument concerning my stance. Authentic faith can stand up to that degree of scrutiny, while mystical faith crumbles at any level of rational investigation. Mystical faith contradicts reason and is not concerned with the need to be defended. This aberrant perspective of faith can be better categorized as wishful thinking or make-believe.

How to Grow Authentic Faith

Authentic faith is grounded in the revelation of the Scriptures and the promise of Christ regarding your destiny. Authentic faith is powerful, yielding results that last, because it keeps on growing with time and experience. Paul commended the church at Thessalonica because he had observed that their faith was "growing more and more" (2 Thess. 1:3). Their faith wasn't something that fell down on them out of the heavens, and it wasn't simply imparted to them through the laying on of hands. It had grown in each and every believer as they dealt with the practical obstacles of this life. We commonly use the phrase "growing in faith," but really it is faith that God is growing in us.

People cannot turn their hope and their confession on and off simply by deciding to do so. The kind of faith described as "the *hypostasis* of things *elpizo*" does not so quickly turn on and off. It does not appear without effort and experience, but neither does it wither in the face of opposition. This is one of the primary things the Holy Spirit is doing in our

71

lives—growing this kind of faith. In fact, it is more central to God's purpose for a person's life than a hundred other things that take a prominent place on the usual prayer list. You want to know what God is up to concerning your life? That's it, growing faith. So then, how do we cultivate faith in our lives so that it grows to be "the *hypostasis* of things *elpizo*"—the very substance and assurance of things hoped for? Following are four basic ways.

1. Faith Comes by Hearing God's Word

Christianity is cognitive; it's for people who think hard about what they believe. More important than whether you have faith like a mountain or faith like a mustard seed is the *content* of your faith. How much you believe is not nearly as important as *what* you believe and the fact that there are good grounds for your faith. That is the context of Paul's exhortation, "Faith comes from hearing the message, and the message is heard through the word of Christ" (Rom. 10:17).

Christians are not asked to put their faith in the private revelations of some ancient or modern spiritual leader. Our faith is based not on myth and legend but on actual events in history. Early Christian preaching was filled with references to what God had actually done in history—how he called Abraham, rescued his people from bondage in Egypt, and raised Jesus from the dead.

Christianity is based on hundreds and thousands of eyewitness accounts of the life, death, burial, and resurrection of Christ. Every time the gospel is preached in the book of

Acts, it is accompanied by the phrase "And we are witnesses of these things!" Many of those witnesses gave their lives for a faith that was based on what they saw with their own eyes. The accurate account of the words of Christ himself was validated by those who spent three years with him.

So you see, Christian faith is rooted and grounded in truth, evidence, and history. It is as though Jesus has said to the world just what he said to Thomas: "Put your finger here; see my hands. Reach out your hand and put it into my side. Stop doubting and believe" (John 20:27).

How different this is from the crazy idea that it doesn't matter what you believe, just as long as your faith is strong. Christian faith is not just a matter of getting all worked up and inspired to believe great and lofty things. There has to be a historical-theological basis for your faith, your hope, and your belief. That basis for truth is in the Word of God.

2. Faith Grows by Hearing God's Voice

"Why doesn't God ever speak to me?" A lot of people ask that question, and on numerous occasions, so have I. There is probably not a single or a simple answer. I think, however, that it is safe to say that the problem for most of us is that we are either too distracted to hear or too busy to wait. We have the TV on constantly, we have the CD player on auto repeat, we hang out with our friends, we have constant activities, our kids are screaming and running around, and we're wired to the Internet. In the midst of doing five different things at the same time, we ask the question, Why doesn't God speak to me? When a rare opportunity for quiet time presents itself, we're just too wound up to sit still. We can't handle the silence and inactivity.

Have you ever gotten so tired of the busyness of life or so desperate for direction that you just took off for a weekend sabbatical? I have. I've locked myself in a hotel room and declared that I would not come out until I had heard from God. Having fasted, prayed, sung, and cried out, I finally went home frustrated and a little angry. How could God be so inconsiderate? I used my hard-earned money to rent a hotel room, canceled my appointments, and even missed the play-off game on TV. Then I had to go home and answer questions from my wife and church associates who were eager to hear what God had said to me.

"So what did the Lord say, David?"

"Well," I replied, not really wanting to talk about it, "nothing."

I'm certainly not suggesting we shouldn't go away to seek the Lord. I think, however, that we often ask God to fit himself into our schedule and our agenda. We need an answer to a particular question, our deadline is within ten business days, and we have scheduled the first weekend in November to get that answer from the Lord. With such effort, planning, and sacrifice on our part, surely God should answer. How dare he not?

There are several reasons I didn't hear from God as I had hoped on my little weekend sabbatical. One is that I was so wrapped up in the importance of my own schedule that I tried to fit his purposes into my timetable. I've got news for you. In God's economy there is no such thing as chronological time, at least as we know it. Though he does accomplish things for us in our space-time world, he's always more concerned about his planned purpose for our lives than he is about the clock or the calendar. As the saying goes, "God's never in a hurry, but he's always on time."

Have you ever noticed that when people are born again, suddenly they "know that they know that they know" that they have been forgiven and that Christ lives in their heart? They don't know how they know, but they have an assurance beyond their understanding.

The apostle Paul wrote in his letter to the Romans, "The Spirit Himself bears witness with our spirit that we are children of God, and if children, heirs also, heirs of God and fellow heirs with Christ" (Rom. 8:16–17 NASB). The full assurance of faith, the inner confidence beyond understanding, the substance of things hoped for, the "*hypostasis* of things *elpizo*," comes as the result of fellowshiping with the Holy Spirit.

3. Faith Grows by Standing on God's Promises

The very nature of our covenant with God establishes conviction about the promises we hope for. God has bound himself to his promises. He honors what he has promised us. I know a lot of good church people who are looking for a prophecy to confirm and support the things they hope for. My advice is to look not so much for the *prophecy* but for the *promise* in God's Word. Prophecy can indeed provide direction, exhortation, or encouragement. However, it will never replace the assurance that comes from resting our hope in the promise of God's Word that is received by faith alone in Christ.

Paul wrote that the certain assurance was for "those who are of the faith of Abraham." That kind of faith is described in the following verses:

> Against all hope, Abraham in hope believed and so became the father of many nations, just as it had been said to him, "So shall your offspring be." Without weakening in his faith, he faced the fact that his body was as good as dead—since he was about a hundred years old—and that Sarah's womb was also dead. Yet he did not waver through unbelief regarding the promise of God, but was strengthened in his faith and gave glory to God, being fully persuaded that God had power to do what he had promised.
>
> Romans 4:18–21

God changed Abram's name to Abraham, which means "father of many nations." God's spoken promise to him included the fact that he would be the father of many nations. Abraham stood in faith without wavering, and what did he become? Exactly what God promised he would be. It works the same way for each one of us with regard to the promises of God's Word and the promises he has spoken to us.

It is important to note that Abraham didn't come up with this plan on his own. He was happy living in Ur and had perhaps reconciled himself to having no children through Sarah. The departure from Ur, the Promised Land of Canaan, and the great nation from his seed—all this was God's idea. The reason Abraham possessed a fully assured faith that maintained hope against all hope was that he based it all on *God's* calling and promise and not on his own desires. It was a practical application of what the apostle Paul wrote many years later: "Faith comes from hearing the message, and the message is heard through the word of Christ" (Rom. 10:17).

Standing on a promise against all odds is not easy. However, along with God's promise and God's calling comes a supernatural assurance of faith. In fact, one way to test God's calling or a personal promise outside his written Word is to look for evidence of his grace. That grace may take the form of divinely orchestrated circumstances or supernatural provision, or it may be in the form of the extraordinary ability to believe with full assurance, even to hope against hope. Endeavoring to emulate the faith of Abraham, I contemplate the present realities without wavering in unbelief with respect to the promise of God.

4. Faith Grows through Exercise

I attended several organizational leadership classes while completing my doctoral program. We had some visiting professors who explained leadership theories from all over the world. Frankly, it was mind-numbing. Then a professor came in one day and introduced himself by saying, "I'm a practitioner. I don't just *study* leadership; I *do* leadership." That got my attention, and I connected with everything he said.

If you are looking for that kind of practical, down-to-earth theology, you will love the book of James. James wasn't a theorist who dealt with complex doctrine and theology; he was a practitioner. Listen to James's practical application of faith: "What use is it, my brethren, if a man says he has faith, but he has no works? Can that faith save him? . . . Faith, if it has no works, is dead, being by itself" (James 2:14, 17 NASB).

What is the work or evidence of faith? It is the *exercising* of faith. The verses following could be read like this: "Faith, if there is no exercising of it, is dead, being by itself. But someone may well say, 'You have faith, and I exercise faith; show me your faith without exercising it, and I will show you my faith by the way I exercise it. . . . But are you willing to recognize, you foolish fellow, that faith without exercising it is useless?" (James 2:17–20, paraphrased).

Faith is like a muscle. Exercise it and it grows stronger. Gradually increase the weight, and over a long period of consistent exercise, you'll become stronger than you ever thought you could be. Likewise, lesser efforts produce less growth. With little or no effort, atrophy sets in. If your faith is ever to grow into the kind of unshakable assurance spoken of in Hebrews 11:1, you have to exercise it. Your faith has to be expressed in action.

Don't miss the significance of the verbs, the action words, in the writer's description of faith in Hebrews 11. By faith Abel *offered sacrifices,* by faith Noah *warned,* by faith Abraham *obeyed,* by faith Isaac *blessed,* by faith Joseph *gave orders,* and so on. The writer identifies faith with action, and he interprets action as faith. In the words of James, these heroes and heroines showed their faith by their works.

September 11, 2001, will go down in history as a day of infamy for our nation. Four planes were hijacked: two crashed into the World Trade Center, a third crashed into the Pentagon, and the fourth was headed for either the

Capitol or the White House but crashed in an open field in Pennsylvania.

Passenger Todd Beamer, a thirty-two-year-old father of two and a dedicated Christian, was on that fourth flight "which was actually a United flight out of Newark [New Jersey] that was going to San Francisco."[4] He was a graduate of Wheaton College and a member of the Princeton Alliance Church in Princeton, New Jersey. Todd Beamer managed to telephone a GTE operator and tell her that the plane had been hijacked. Having heard what had happened within the previous few hours, Todd had no doubt where they were headed and for what purpose.

Beamer told the operator that he had gathered several men. They prayed the Lord's Prayer together, and the last thing the operator heard was Beamer saying, "Okay, let's roll." We don't know exactly what happened after that. Apparently the hijackers were overcome, but in the process the plane crashed.

Todd Beamer could have simply organized a prayer meeting in the back of the plane. They could have engaged in spiritual warfare, "binding" and "loosing" and "interceding." But in this case, Beamer put his faith into action.

If you want your faith to grow, you can't simply sit back and watch. Like Todd Beamer, you must find some way to exercise your faith. Begin to do something. What is it that you have been believing God for? What is it you want to accomplish in life? What is it God has promised you? Don't be spineless, don't be lethargic, don't give up in the face of questions. Move forward as a child of God saying, "God, I am going to lay hold of your promise, I am going to believe that you will do what you said you would do, and I am going to act on that faith. Even though I may despair or at times lose courage, I'm going to stand in your strength, in your ability, and not my own frailty. I will lay hold of your promises and watch what you will do."

five

STORMS OFFER LESSONS
IN FAITH

ow many times have you felt like a sinking disciple? These are the times when you face the
most critical and fearful moments of your life
and you have to fight like mad to stay afloat. During such
times it seems the Lord is distant and unconcerned about
your situation. You think to yourself, *The Lord may be with
me, but he's asleep in the back of my boat.* And at that point
you do everything you can to awaken God.

There is a precious couple in my congregation who after
eleven years of marriage were unable to have a child of their
own. After suffering a miscarriage and enduring various

fertility treatments and medical operations, Marguerita and Richard Gooding did not receive the answer to their prayers. In their capacity as associate pastors, working alongside me for many years, I have seen them encouraging and praying with other couples who also wanted to have children. And I have seen them rejoice when God answered others' prayers and children were conceived. Yet their personal cry seemed to go unheard.

After working through the maze of disappointment in this area of their lives, the Goodings turned their attention toward adoption. And even that seemed to be emotionally challenging and wrought with false starts and dashed hopes. Both Richard and Marguerita were at the point of crying out, "Lord, don't you care that we are perishing?" At this lowest point in their faith, the Goodings received a call from the adoption agency with the news that a three-week-old baby girl was available for adoption. When they called me to share the good news, all I could hear were screams of joy, and I knew the ordeal was over.

Jesus's disciples found themselves in a similar situation. The Lord had spent all day teaching a multitude beside the Sea of Galilee. When evening came, he said to his disciples, "Let's go over to the other side." And so they set sail. During their night crossing, a storm came upon them with such ferocity that the waves were breaking over the sides of the boat and it was quickly filling with water. It would only be a few moments until they all sank to their deaths. The disciples were no doubt fighting for their lives, throwing overboard any cargo they were carrying and frantically bailing water. And what was Jesus doing all this time? He was in the back of the boat, presumably in some kind of cabin or shelter, asleep. Finally some of the disciples woke up their master and asked, "Teacher, do You not care that we are perishing?" (Mark 4:38 NASB).

Looking at History

It is not unusual for modern-day Christians to have a romanticized view of the first-century church and of first-century Christians. When we take a closer look, however, we find that early Christians also struggled with faith, desperately needed encouragement, and even contemplated giving up. Just like you and me, they were people with hopes and dreams, fears and uncertainties. When we find portions of Scripture specifically written to people whose faith was on the verge of collapse, those passages strengthen us in the midst of our own trials.

Think about the examples in Hebrews 11—Noah building the ark for 120 years; Abraham trusting God for a son even at age seventy-five; Moses leading a nation from captivity through the Red Sea. What these people displayed was not your garden variety of faith. These are examples of people whose faith was wavering on the verge of disintegration, but despite their suffering they hung on to faith and ultimately saw God do exactly what he had promised.

The writer of Hebrews is not simply expounding theology. He is writing directly to people hanging on to faith by their fingertips. "Do not throw away your confidence," he writes. "You need to persevere" (10:35–36). They needed hope and encouragement as much as anyone.

83

There is usually more than one way to interpret the meaning of New Testament narratives. You have to consider what actually happened, what it meant to those present, and what it means for us today. For the disciples, the experience of seeing Jesus asleep in the boat while their lives were in jeopardy was a turning point in their relationship with Jesus. Up to that point, they saw him as a great teacher and a prophet equal to John the Baptist, and even to the great prophet Elijah. Though it is not clear from the preceding chapters that they had yet come to think of Jesus as the Jewish Messiah, they had witnessed him casting out demons, healing people with sicknesses, and preaching to vast multitudes. Then came this incident, a great storm in the middle of the night on the Sea of Galilee. Mark records what happened: "And being aroused, He [Jesus] rebuked the wind and said to the sea, 'Hush, be still.' And the wind died down and it became perfectly calm" (Mark 4:40 NASB).

Although I have been to the Sea of Galilee on tours of the Holy Land, I can't imagine what that experience was like for them. In a single moment there arose a raging wind on the sea with huge waves breaking over the boat. Then Jesus woke up and had a few words with the wind and the sea, and suddenly everything was perfectly calm. That must have been mind-boggling for the disciples. To say they had a paradigm shift is putting it mildly. In those brief moments, the disciples realized that Jesus did not fit into any of their previously understood historical or theological categories. He was not simply a teacher or a prophet. And he certainly was not what they expected the Messiah to be. Jesus was uniquely above and beyond any man who had ever lived. You can sense their astonishment and bewilderment in Mark 4:41: "They became very much afraid and said to one another, 'Who then is this, that even the wind and the sea obey Him?'" (NASB).

Facing the Storms of Life

What does this story say to us today, and how can we apply it as we face our own storms? The answer is found in the words Jesus said to his frightened disciples: "Why are you so timid? How is it that you have no faith?" (Mark 4:40 NASB). Now those are two good questions to think about. Here I am, in the middle of the sea, in the middle of the night, in the middle of a fierce gale that is about to sink the ship I'm standing on. Why am I afraid, and how is it that I don't have faith? Several answers come to mind. Namely, the wind, the waves, the sinking, and most of all the likelihood of drowning. What must have equally astounded the disciples was that Jesus's questions implied that he expected them *not* to doubt or be fearful in such situations. He also must expect the same of us. And at that I too am astounded.

The calming of the storm was a great faith lesson for the disciples. What does it teach us? There are four things we can learn from the story: (1) There is always another side, (2) you cannot take everyone with you, (3) you should expect storms, and (4) Jesus speaks to us in the storms.

Lesson 1: There Is Always Another Side

The first step in growing in faith is when you realize there is another side. That means you do not have to stay

85

the way you are. You do not have to accept everything that comes your way. You do not have to be a victim. You do not have to be someone whom life beats up. You do not have to live with your dreams and God's promises unfulfilled. There is always another side, a better side, and Jesus said, "Let's go over there."

That means you can have a better marriage, a stronger marriage, a better relationship with your parents, a better relationship with your kids. God will enable you to climb the ladder to another level of success. He will enable you to do things that are more meaningful in your family, in your ministry, in attaining your calling. There is always another side, a better side, replete with promises that can be attained. That again is the theme of Hebrews, which teaches that by the new covenant in Christ, we have a better reward, a better promise, a better inheritance.

Lesson 2: You Cannot Take Everyone with You

On the subject of faith and trusting in God's ability to provide, noted author Corrie ten Boom wrote, "The Lord is not only my shepherd; He is my treasurer. He is very wealthy. Sometimes He tries my faith, but when I am obedient then the money always comes in just in time."[1]

I live in a high mountainous area of New Jersey that is prone to foggy mornings. Whenever the fog descends on the landscape, I have to pick my way carefully while driving. And it affirms Corrie ten Boom's words, helping me understand that although I can hardly see the road ahead, by faith (and my familiarity with the road) I keep moving slowly through the fog until I reach my destination. It is always interesting to see the reaction of unfamiliar passengers riding with me. They grip their seat tightly, thinking I'm going to crash at any given moment. Because they can't see the road ahead, their fear makes them lose confidence and faith in my driving. Likewise, when working your way to the other side in faith, not everyone with you will be willing to take the journey.

Matthew, in his account of the story of Jesus calming the storm (Matt. 8:18–27), says that as soon as Jesus had given the order to depart for the other side, two men came up wanting to follow him wherever he went. One was a scribe, apparently a religious leader whose heart was not right. Jesus turned him away. The other man wanted to follow, but with certain conditions. He had responsibilities at home. Jesus told him, "Follow Me; and allow the dead to bury their own dead" (v. 22 NASB). So Jesus and his disciples departed from the anxious multitude alone.

When crossing over to the other side of faith, to the better side, you cannot force others to come with you. Many will not want to go. Yet your departure should not be based on the willingness of others. If you are going to make a decision to follow Jesus and make a commitment to a walk of faith, you cannot wait for a vote of confidence from your friends, family, business associates, or classmates. You may have to go it alone.

Some people don't go deeper in their relationship with Christ and are not bolder in their faith because they are overly concerned about what others may think of them. Many husbands secretly harbor the desire to become the spiritual head of the family but are afraid that their wives will criticize them because of lukewarm commitments the husbands have made in the past. Similarly, some wives want to grow spiritually and become bolder in their faith but are concerned about how their husbands will react. They say they want to "go over to a better side," but they fear creating tension at home.

Sadly, the people who hesitate because of the fear of tension in the home do so because there is *already* tension in the home. Usually there is a self-centered, unbelieving partner or unresolved conflicts in the marriage. The more Christ-centered, Spirit-indwelled, and faith-filled the marriage, the greater the love, joy, and peace will be. It stands to reason that a person's decision to stand more boldly in faith and to follow Christ more diligently will provoke opposition and even persecution in the marriage. That can indeed happen. And in the short run, the road may become rocky. However, becoming more committed to following Christ is the only medicine to heal the true source of tension at home. The alternative is to stand on the shoreline and watch others cross over to the other side.

Lesson 3: You Should Expect Storms

The storm hit not long after they decided to go over to the other side. Maybe the clouds were gathering even as they shoved off, and that's why no other boats followed. In any case, the story is symbolic of what often happens when people make a decision to follow Jesus by faith to the other side, the better side. Sometimes you follow him right into a storm.

Don't be surprised if storm clouds begin to form when you decide that you'll apply for that promotion. Or when you finally summon up the courage to go back to school to get that degree. Or when you make a commitment to pray and stand in faith for a family member or to increase your giving. Invariably a storm will arise.

When a young man commits himself to serve God, it's not unusual that the beautiful, seductive girl whom he had been desperately trying to impress suddenly decides to give him a call. Even though he had previously done everything possible to win her affections with no sign of progress, she suddenly gains a new interest in him. The corresponding reality is equally true for women who decide to follow Christ. It is also true for people who decide to stop drinking because they believe God has something better for them. Suddenly they are offered free drinks everywhere they go.

I don't want to discourage you from taking a step of faith, because it does not *always* happen this way. But don't be shocked if it does. Listen to what Peter wrote: "Do not be surprised at the fiery ordeal among you, which comes upon you for your testing, as though some strange thing were happening to you" (1 Pet. 4:12 NASB).

Somewhere along the way many of us have adopted the idea that if God is really with us, and that if he is really for us, and if we are really called, and if we are really walking in his will, and really standing in faith, then we win the prize of a storm-free life. Sometimes pastors reinforce that idea, especially in churches where people are commonly asked to share personal testimonies. We line up all the exciting stories that have quick, happy endings. Yet the brother or sister who stepped out in faith and right into a hurricane may not be asked to share in the public meeting.

Remember that it was Jesus's idea to go to the other side, and the disciples had the Son of God himself, in the flesh, sleeping in the back of their boat. Storms may come, but those too are part of God's plan. They are his way of getting us to the better side.

Lesson 4: Jesus Speaks to Us in the Storms

Robert and Maria (pseudonyms), cherished members of my congregation, related to me how they were able to overcome a stormy season in their lives through faith. For years, Maria had experienced severe panic attacks and had become terrified about leaving the house—even to apply for a driver's license. Although this illness had slight flare-ups during her teenage years, the sickness intensified shortly after she and Robert were married, and she began taking medication to stabilize her emotions. Maria was bound and didn't know how to discover freedom.

Robert, a new believer in Christ, desperately wanted to see his wife experience a full life but did not know what to do. Finally Maria too came to know Christ as her Savior, but she remained deathly afraid of venturing outside of her immediate neighborhood to find a church.

As God would have it, Maria and Robert found our congregation, Christ Church, which at the time was located less than five minutes from their home. After their second visit to the church, the Holy Spirit used me to pray with Maria about key areas of her life at the close of the service.

The prayer focused on Maria receiving strength from God to overcome all kinds of fears she was battling. According to Robert, that very day she stopped taking the mood-enhancing medicine. Since that time, over twelve years ago, Maria has not taken even one more dose.

However, there is a second part to her miracle that occurred through the exercise of their faith. As a result of seeing the power of prayer, Robert gained a new infusion of faith to seek Maria's complete healing. After he cried out to the Lord in prayer for a few days, the Holy Spirit impressed upon Robert's heart to confront his deep, dark secret of pornography. This young man was secretly involved in pornography, and his sinful activity was being done in different parts of the home, including the bathroom. After being convicted of his behavior, Robert privately cried out to God for a strategy to combat by faith what he suddenly realized might be affecting his wife's emotional state.

Robert was quite serious about his need for deliverance from pornography and his wife's healing. So he took off two weeks from work and fasted for the entire length of time. His strategy incorporated a number of different components, including having a friend anoint him with oil for a breakthrough. He also confessed his bondage to Maria, and she forgave him, telling him that she was unaware of his addiction and that she would support him in his quest for freedom.

At the end of the first week of fasting, Robert was in his backyard when the thought suddenly came to him to adopt Joshua's battle plan against Jericho as his faith strategy against pornography. Each of the seven days of the following week, Robert marched around his house as Joshua marched around the walls of Jericho (cf. Joshua 6). On the seventh day, after marching around his house, Robert shouted at the top of his voice the praises of God, and he experienced the breakthrough of his life. Despite the neighbors' stares and what they must have thought of him, Robert conveyed his request for freedom to God and in faith believed that it had occurred.

Robert also said that when he went back inside his house, the heaviness that had loomed over the home was gone. It was powerfully apparent that whatever oppression had been there before was gone. And Maria experienced freedom from panic attacks that very day.

Shortly after that day, Maria received her driver's license and now leaves the home any time she chooses—even taking all kinds of adventurous road trips in response to her newfound deliverance from panic attacks. As a pastor, I celebrate the freedom and victory Robert and Maria gained through their faith in God's ability to take them through the storms of life.

Your Victory Is on the Way

What does the Lord have to say about your situation? Storms of life that try your faith should drive you deeper into your relationship with Christ. They push you to a place where you would probably not go on your own. I've never heard anyone say, "Just as I was making my tenth million dollars, I suddenly realized that I needed faith in God." What I have heard people say is, "I lost my job, and I had to learn to trust

God." Did the million-dollar man need faith? Did he need a closer relationship with Christ? Did he need to hear from God? Yes, but he may have been totally unaware of these needs. Yet I have never had to encourage people who were in the midst of a storm to pray. They were acutely aware of their need for God's presence, help, and direction.

There is nothing in this world I would rather be than the pastor of Christ Church in New Jersey. However, being in the ministry does not exempt one from trials. On the contrary, it is more like being turned into a trial magnet. The apostle Paul would be the first to say amen to that. You deal with the trials that teach you humility, trials that teach you lessons so that you can relate to people, trials that are the attacks of Satan, and more trials that teach you lessons to preach because you have to preach a lot. Then, when you're done learning those lessons, you gain the burden of everyone else's personal trials in the congregation.

After several years of trials and storms, the most important lesson I have learned is how to listen for God's voice during these times of testing. I used to respond to wind and waves crashing over the sides of my boat by crying out, "Lord, don't you care that I am perishing?" Now my prayer is more likely to be, "Okay, Lord, what do you want to do in my life? What do you want to say to me through this situation? What do you want me to do?"

Instead of questioning God's concern or simply asking him to make the storm go away, I ask God what strategy I should follow. "Lord, give me insight, give me foresight, give me some kind of practical, logistical steps I can take that will help me through this predicament." After that prayer, I start looking and listening for God to speak.

That is what Jesus's disciples learned. God's specific word of wisdom to you might be to cast your net on the other side of the boat, as he told his disciples who had fished all night and caught nothing. It could be similar to what God said to the people through Moses, "Stand by and see the salvation of the LORD" (Exod. 14:13 NASB). When faced with a great need for food, Jesus told his disciples to gather what was available and to bring it to him. At the wedding feast in Cana, his mother simply said, "Whatever He says to you, do it" (John 2:5 NASB). In every case, what his followers did out of obedience was an essential key to the miracle.

Seek God for Wisdom

James, in his discussion about enduring trials, writes:

> But if any of you lacks wisdom, let him ask of God, who gives to all men generously and without reproach, and it will be given him. But let him ask in faith without any doubting, for the one who doubts is like the surf of the sea driven and tossed by the wind. For let not that man expect that he will receive anything from the Lord.
>
> James 1:5–7 NASB

In other words, if you are in the midst of a storm, you will be driven by the wind and waves until you get God's wisdom.

94

At times in the Bible, God spoke audibly during people's trials. Some, like Robert and Maria, have testified of that same experience. Most of the time, though, God speaks to us through an inward voice. Sometimes he puts a thought into my mind to read a particular book, and in it I find his direction. Then there are other times when God simply impresses upon our hearts what we are to do.

You cannot expect to discover God's strategy without seeking him in prayer and meditation. It would be a lot easier to go to your pastor or to another wise Christian counselor for his or her advice. These people can certainly help, but they cannot vicariously seek God for you. You have to carve out the time to seek him for his specific strategy for your individual trial yourself.

When the angel Gabriel announced the birth of Jesus to Mary, his concluding remarks were, "Nothing will be impossible with God" (Luke 1:37 NASB). The literal translation reads, "*Not any word* will be impossible with God." To put it another way, nothing that God speaks to you will be impossible. Trust him to speak to your heart about the best strategy to handle your present trial, and he will comfort you.

six

⁓

RIDING OUT THE STORMS
OF LIFE

Have you ever noticed that once a thought gathers momentum in your mind, it's hard to stop it? If the thought is intense and is allowed to progress long enough, it can snowball, affecting areas of your life that have little to do with the thought on which you're dwelling. This is how some phobias and compulsive behaviors begin and completely overtake a person's life. If you don't take your own thoughts captive, they will eventually captivate you. Habits of the mind are created just like any other habits. If you discipline yourself to think and react in certain patterns, in time those responses are conditioned biologically, psychologically, and spiritually. In biblical terminology, your entire person is to be "sanctif[ied] . . . spirit, soul, and body" (1 Thess. 5:23).

When you fear that the worst will happen, your own thoughts may help bring it about. Someone once wrote, "Fear is the wrong use of imagination. It is anticipating the worst, not the best that can happen."[1]

A salesman, driving on a lonely country road one dark and rainy night, had a flat tire. He opened the trunk—no lug wrench. The light from a farmhouse could be seen dimly up the road. He set out on foot through the driving rain. Surely the farmer would have a lug wrench he could borrow, he thought. Of course, it was late at night—the farmer would be asleep in his warm, dry bed. Maybe he wouldn't answer the door. And even if he did, he'd be angry at being awakened in the middle of the night.

The salesman, picking his way blindly in the dark, stumbled on. By now his shoes and clothing were soaked. Even if the farmer did answer his knock, he would probably shout something like, "What's the big idea waking me up at this hour?" This thought made the salesman angry. What right did that farmer have to refuse him the loan of a lug wrench? After all, here he was stranded in the middle of nowhere, soaked to the skin. The farmer was a selfish clod—no doubt about that!

The salesman finally reached the house and banged loudly on the door. A voice called out, "Who is it?"

His face white with anger, the salesman called out, "You know good and well who it is. It is me! And you can keep your stupid lug wrench. I wouldn't borrow it now if you had the last one on earth!"[2]

Like the traveling salesman, we build up imaginary realities that impact our thinking and behavior. This is why Paul instructed the Corinthians to take every thought captive to the obedience of Christ (2 Cor. 10:5), and why he taught the Philippians to think on things that are true, noble, right, pure, lovely, and admirable (Phil. 4:8).

Thoughts to Remember

When you find yourself in a difficult situation that challenges your faith, you have to examine your thoughts and take captive the ones that cause you to fear or doubt. Don't allow fear or doubt to enslave your mind. Follow Paul's prescription by thinking on things that are lovely. You may think there's nothing lovely about your trial.

But here are four phrases attributed to Andrew Murray, a Christian writer, which I stumbled upon while surfing the Internet one day. Whenever you are facing times of despair, you must learn to say (1) I am here by God's appointment, (2) I am here in God's keeping, (3) I am here under God's training, and (4) I am here in God's timing. Let me elaborate on their meaning and provide illustrations.

1. I Am Here by God's Appointment

When thrown into prison in Rome, Paul wrote back to the Philippian church, "What has happened to me has really served to advance the gospel" (Phil. 1:12). When there was a financial need, he said that one person's need is an opportunity for another's generosity (2 Corinthians 8).

The weakness in the body of Christ exists so that we will be dependent on one another (1 Corinthians 12). That was always Paul's approach. To him there was no such thing as a setback. He was always on the offensive. Whatever happened, he assumed it was somehow designed for the greater progress of the gospel.

But what if they simply killed Paul; *that* couldn't be a good thing, could it? You would think not; however, Paul wrote, "Christ will be exalted in my body, whether by life or by death" (Phil. 1:20). Paul's perspective was, *The worst thing they can do to me is kill me, and then I win.* How do you deal with someone like that?

One of the most famous passages in the Bible is from Paul's letter to the Romans, in which he wrote, "We know that in all things God works for the good of those who love him, who have been called according to his purpose" (8:28). Many of the sermons preached in American pulpits either refer to or are based on the theology of that verse. Unfortunately, we rarely consider its context. Look at the verses following that text with regard to the commitment to holding a healthy perspective and a positive attitude in the midst of trials:

> What then shall we say to these things? If God is for us, who is against us? . . . Who shall separate us from the love of Christ? Shall tribulation, or distress, or persecution, or famine, or nakedness, or peril, or sword? Just as it is written,
> "For Thy sake we are being put to death all day long;
> We were considered as sheep to be slaughtered."

100

But in all these things we overwhelmingly conquer through Him who loved us. For I am convinced that neither death, nor life, nor angels, nor principalities, nor things present, nor things to come, nor powers, nor height, nor depth, nor any other created thing, shall be able to separate us from the love of God, which is in Christ Jesus our Lord.

Romans 8:31, 35–39 NASB

Paul supports the positive reality of verse 28 with a litany of other possible experiences that may hurt but not cripple the faith of a person walking in faith. When I read Romans 8:28–39, it seems as if God himself comes down from heaven and personally reassures me, saying, *"David, whatever painful thing you're going through, I have given you the resiliency to bounce back again. Don't worry!"* This scriptural reassurance helps to form the foundation for saying and believing that during life's storms I am here by God's appointment.

After facilitating the deliverance of a teenage girl from demonic spirits, Paul and Silas were thrown into prison. After they performed this wonderful act for the teenage fortune-teller, the girl's masters' inability to profit thereafter put the two apostles in a terrible trial—prison (Acts 16:23–25). Contrary to what most people would do after being publicly humiliated, stripped, and beaten, these men of God started singing songs to God.

Though things had turned out badly for Paul and Silas, their praise and worship are evidence that they were still able to say, "We are here by God's appointment." And if you follow their example, you eliminate the possibility of viewing yourself as a victim, no matter how great the injustice

101

or pain. When you say, "I am here by God's appointment," you defeat the emotions that cause you to feel that your tough circumstances are a sign that God no longer loves you. If you start out this way, the natural response is not to complain, but to be found singing hymns of praise and to say with Paul that in everything you will be victorious.

2. I Am Here in God's Keeping

"Suddenly there was such a violent earthquake that the foundations of the prison were shaken. At once all the prison doors flew open and everybody's chains came loose" (Acts 16:26). Paul and Silas were praying and singing hymns because they trusted that they were in that jail by God's appointment and that they were there in his keeping. Obviously it wasn't because they knew *what* was about to happen but because they knew *who* was in control. In other words, they were not appointed to that jail merely by the authority of the Philippian magistrates or by the power of the jail or the jailer. You can see that same attitude in Jesus as he stood before Pilate and said, "You would have no power over me if it were not given to you from above" (John 19:11).

I have heard people exhort others to give praise as a means of getting God's attention and getting him to move on their behalf. I am not certain that approach is completely accurate. I do realize that there is such a form of prayer commonly referred to as the prayer of adoration (praise). However, I am pretty sure about this: Paul and Silas were not praying and singing hymns of praise to get God's attention or to persuade him to take control. Even though they were beaten, bleeding, and sitting in a prison with their feet in stocks, they praised God because they believed they were *already* in his keeping and that he was indeed in control.

Maybe you are in a mess with absolutely no way out. You cannot break your chains or escape your prison. You just need to trust that you are there by God's appointment and that you are there in God's keeping. This perspective is not a hopeless or faithless view. Rather, it is a true faith response. Like Paul and Silas, you must learn to have faith in God's providence and sovereignty even though you don't understand what he is doing or how your trial can help you.

The great Baptist preacher Charles Spurgeon once preached what in his judgment was one of his poorest sermons. He stammered and floundered, and when he got through he felt that it had been a complete failure. He was greatly humiliated, and when he got home he fell on his knees and said, "Lord, God, Thou canst do something with nothing. Bless that poor sermon."

All through the week he uttered that prayer. He woke up in the night and prayed about it. He determined that the next Sunday he would redeem himself by preaching a great sermon. Sure enough, the next Sunday the sermon went off beautifully. At the close of the service, the people crowded around him and covered him with praise.

Spurgeon went home pleased with himself, and that night he slept like a baby. But he said to himself, "I'll watch the results of those two sermons." What were they? From the one that had seemed a failure, he was able to trace forty-one conversions. And from that "magnificent" sermon, he was unable to discover that a single soul was saved. The Spirit of God used the one but not the other.[3]

In the midst of your ordeal, learn to make this confession: I am here in God's keeping. More important than the phrase is the attitude and inner resolve that God is able to make something good out of that which seems so unsuccessful.

3. I Am Here under God's Training

According to a legend, a king once placed a heavy stone in the roadway. Then he hid and waited to see who would remove it. Many who came by loudly blamed the government for not keeping the highways clear, but none assumed the duty of pushing the obstacle out of the way. At last a poor peasant stopped and rolled the stone into the ditch beside the road. To his surprise he found a bag full of gold embedded in the road on the spot where the rock had been. A note said it was the king's reward for anyone who removed the troublesome object.

The apostle Peter also wrote that underneath your problems there is indeed a bag of gold. He addresses believers under stress: "You, who are protected by the power of God through faith for a salvation ready to be revealed in the last time." Then he adds, "In this [salvation] you greatly rejoice, even though now for a little while, if necessary, you have been distressed by various trials" (1 Pet. 1:4–6 NASB).

How many times have people cried out, "God, how could you let this happen?" I don't want to oversimplify the answer to that question. Sometimes people wander out from under God's protection because of a conscious decision to rebel.

104

Sometimes people reap what they have sown in ignorance or disobedience. But then there are also those times when God deliberately withdraws his protection because, according to Peter, it was necessary.

There are great lessons that God wants us to learn from the difficulties in our lives. I know the temptation is to react, complain, and agonize over our trials and tribulations. Sometimes the hardest thing to do is to step back and take an objective look at ourselves and our situation. Our first inclination is to pray, "God, how could you let this happen?" or "God, please hurry up and deliver me from this situation!" Perhaps what we should be praying is, "God I'm in this trial by your appointment. I'm here under your keeping. And I am here under your training. What lesson do you want me to learn from this?" Sometimes the answer to that question is surprisingly simple. But we will never see it until we are willing to ask.

One of the themes throughout the book of Hebrews is Christ's identification with our humanity. He was made like us in all things to be a merciful high priest who could understand what it is like to be tempted so that he could sympathize with our weaknesses (2:14–17; 4:14–16). He was "tempted in all things as we are, yet without sin" (4:15 NASB). The discipline and training that accompany trials aren't fun, at least in the moment; but that too is an aspect of our lives that Jesus walked through. In chapter 5 the writer says, "Although He was a Son, He learned obedience from the things which He suffered" (v. 8 NASB). I've learned a few things about obedience too, though not necessarily "without sin."

I shared in chapter 2 how two of the jobs I worked after completing my master's degree in engineering were in a spaghetti factory and a Clairol factory. I did not, however, tell you about one of the key lessons I learned while enduring that trial. I learned the joy of obedience. It all came to a head when I answered yes to the Holy Spirit's question, "David, if I call you to work in this job for the rest of your life, will you do it?" My answer was yes. That day I committed to walking in obedience to God's will even if it did not make any sense to me. Although that experience took place some twenty years ago, and other trials have since come and gone, I can honestly say that the experience of working in those factories is where the Lord broke me in the right places so that I would learn the joy of obedience. What will it take for God to break you so that your soul is tamed? The quicker you learn his lessons, the quicker you graduate from the trial.

Did you ever notice that the mechanical instrument in the washing machine that gets the dirt out is called an "agitator"? Have you ever noticed that God brings people into your life whose mission, so it seems, is to be agitators in your life? These are people who by nature do the very things that irritate you the most, and they do them constantly.

When I landed my first engineering job in 1984, Andy, my supervisor, was a professional engineer (a difficult designation to earn). He also held a Ph.D. in engineering and was an adjunct professor at a nearby university. He was smart, talented, and experienced—and he knew it. Whenever he gave me a task to complete, particularly if it involved writing a report to conclude an investigatory project, he would stand over me as I wrote the findings. Often he would laugh at my work and take his red ink pen (not blue or black ink, but *red*) and make all kinds of corrections. I would get so angry that I thought my hair would stand up on end.

One day I finally had enough after months of enduring this ordeal. No, I did not quit the job or tell my supervisor off, though I desperately wanted to. I went out to the nearby bookstore and bought about a dozen books on writing, vowing that I would fix Andy by learning how to write. In hindsight, I realized that God used Andy as an agitator in my life to improve my writing. Just imagine the irony here. The books that I've written, including this one, were made possible because of my agitator, Andy. Through that experience I learned to say, "I am here under God's training."

Take a moment and reflect on some of the trials you have successfully completed. I am sure that in retrospect you can see a pile of lessons you learned along the way. Assume the same pattern holds true in every trial. The present hardship has a new and valued set of teaching points. Exercise your faith by believing in your heart and confessing with your mouth this truth: I am here under God's training.

4. I Am Here in God's Timing

In Acts 16 we learn about a great earthquake that struck around midnight and supernaturally opened the cell doors and freed all the prisoners. The jailer who had been charged with the prisoners' keeping was about to fall on his sword when Paul called to him with a loud voice, "Don't harm yourself! We are all here!" The jailer called for lights and rushed in and fell trembling before Paul and Silas (Acts 16:28–29). You would think that an earthquake that opened all the doors would be the perfect time to run for your life. But it wasn't God's timing for Paul and Silas to leave. They could have been mistaken as fugitives of the law.

The next day the magistrates sent their officers to release Paul and Silas. "Release those men," they ordered. Paul replied, "They beat us publicly without a trial, even though we are Roman citizens, and threw us into prison. And now do they want to get rid of us quietly? No! Let them come themselves and escort us out" (Acts 16:37). The magistrates, who were terrified that they had offended both God and the Roman Empire, went to the prison and begged Paul and Silas to leave the prison and the city. The jailer in charge of their imprisonment was now their disciple and aide. The officers who had beaten them with rods could no longer force them to obey their orders, and the magistrates were at the jail begging for them to leave peacefully. What a great reversal! With that, Paul and Silas determined that it was God's time to be delivered.

Not only does God have a purpose and plan for our lives, he has his own timetable. In Philippi Paul was delivered from prison almost immediately. In Ephesus he spent two years in prison. When a crowd tried to seize Jesus, "no one laid a hand on him, because his time had not yet come" (John 7:30). And when he was given over to his greatest trial, it was because, as Jesus himself said, "My appointed time is near" (Matt. 26:18).

When you are in a trial and have said to yourself, "I am here by God's appointment; I am here under his keeping and his training," you then also have to understand that you are in God's timing. That means you don't know how long your trial is going to last. The trial you are in right now may run for two days, two weeks, two months, or two years. Some trials may last twenty years or a lifetime.

It is important to differentiate between trials that have a definite timing and trials you endure until you learn a lesson. In the latter, the quicker you learn the lesson, the sooner you move out of that situation. If not, a trial that is meant for a period of time can become a lifelong event. After twenty years God may still be dealing with the same issue in your life.

It's like going through elementary school. If you refuse to learn fourth-grade math, you'll get held back. It is a shame to be twenty years old and still be a student in the fourth grade. It's even worse to be wearing diapers and drinking from a bottle at age fifty. We are supposed to learn the lessons and move on in the Lord.

That image reminds me of a passage from Hebrews 5, which Bible scholars call the "peril of unbelief" (5:11–6:20). It begins with these words:

> For though by this time you ought to be teachers, you have need again for someone to teach you the elementary principles of the oracles of God, and you have come to need milk and not solid food. For everyone who partakes only of milk is not accustomed to the word of righteousness, for he is a babe. But solid food is for the mature, who because of practice have their senses trained to discern good and evil. . . . Let us press on to maturity.
>
> Hebrews 5:12–14; 6:1 NASB

The process of building faith is similar to the way pearls are formed. A little grain of sand finds its way into the nucleus of an oyster. To protect itself from the irritating sand, the oyster secretes a crystalline substance that surrounds the grain of sand. This process continues for several years until there is a perfectly formed pearl. Similarly, in your life, even a small irritation can yield a result as beautiful as a pearl.

That crystalline substance we should release during times of irritation is praise and worship. When you begin to worship God and praise him in the midst of your trial, this worship begins a process that will create something beautiful in your life. I love being around seasoned saints because they exude the spiritual equivalent of a fragrant aroma flowing out of their lives. Though they may be going through tough times, they are wonderful to be around because they have learned to say these four things: *I am here by God's appointment . . . I'm here in his keeping . . . I'm here under his training . . .* and *I'm here in his timing.*

When, by faith, you build your life on these four pillars, no matter what you go through, you will always know that God is creating something beautiful in your life through your attitude of faith.

seven

HOW TO APPLY FAITH

T eaching you how to apply faith is sort of like trying to teach you how to drive a car. I can give you the basic rules, but you will learn the most by putting those rules to practice. When my wife and I were teaching our oldest daughter how to drive, we gave Danielle bits of information as the lessons unfolded. We couldn't teach her everything at once. And although over time we gave Danielle much information, it would have taken Marlinda and me a lifetime to give her the full rundown on every possible road condition or weather condition she would face. Not to mention the myriad defensive driving maneuvers she would have to employ to be an excellent, responsible driver. Faith is like that. Certainly I can provide you with the basic guidelines, but the true learning comes in the doing.

The word *faith* is technically a noun, yet it is so dynamic in Scripture that it is given the force of a verb. "Faith" translates the Greek word *pistis*, which means "firm persuasion" and "conviction strong enough to triumph over all obstacles." Drawing from the rich example of faith outlined in Hebrews 11:1–39, the words that describe what each character did to verify faith are all action words.

By faith Abel *offered* God a better sacrifice; Enoch *was taken* from this life; Noah *condemned* the world and *became* heir of the righteousness; Abraham by faith *obeyed and went*. By faith Isaac *blessed* Jacob and Esau; and by faith Jacob *blessed* each of Joseph's sons. By faith Joseph *spoke about* how his bones should be carried out of Egypt upon the exodus of Israel to the Promised Land. By faith Moses *refused* to be known as the son of Pharaoh's daughter any longer. By faith some *conquered* kingdoms, *administered* justice, *gained* what was promised, and *shut the mouths* of lions.

All of the evidences of faith in the lives of these heroes are action based. This means that faith is about *doing* and *being*, not necessarily just about mental assent, or watching and hoping. The inescapable question is, How can I apply such active faith to my situation? This question calls for answers that are practical, down-to-earth, and capable of being implemented by ordinary people.

Five Steps to Applying Faith

There are at least five specific ways to apply authentic and results-oriented faith: (1) Stand on God's Word, (2) apply faith by praying and fasting, (3) listen to the Holy Spirit,

(4) establish a faith confession, and (5) exercise the power of agreement. Let's examine each one.

1. Stand on God's Word

I recently had a dream in which I found myself explaining the Bible's position on marital separation to a man in my congregation. In the dream, it was clear that he and his wife were both Christians, but the husband had been contemplating a separation. When I opened my Bible to 1 Corinthians 7—the famous chapter on biblical separation—the entire page had two inches of grass growing out of it!

I was shocked to see this in my Bible. The grass obscured the entire page. I reached for a pair of scissors and cut the grass away. In a split second the page was as clear and readable as normal. Once I read the applicable verses and interpreted them to the man, his eyes were opened to the fact that he had no grounds for a separation. Rather than becoming angry at the standard of God's Word, or trying to find a loophole to wriggle through, the man was able to see that the flip side of God's standard was a wonderful promise.

In this case, God's promise is this: *Stay together and I will help you work through your conflict to achieve harmony and peace through faith.* I awakened from the dream with the realization once again that God's Word is chock-full of promises awaiting our discovery. And once we understand the Word's intent, desires, safeguards, and promises, we have the basis to trust implicitly in its truthfulness.

To stand on God's Word means to believe its promises for your life. In the case of the man in my dream, he planned to act in the most convenient way possible, until he heard the Bible's guidelines for marital separation. Once he became aware of God's position, he quickly adjusted his actions and decisions to stay with his wife. He made a 180-degree change to get in sync with God's expressed wisdom outlined in the Bible. In other words, he recognized that God's promises and provisions are obtained by adhering to the will of God expressed in the Word of God. This is what it means to stand on God's Word: *To believe his promises by coming under the government and rule of the Scriptures.*

A significant mistake that the Israelites made following their exodus from Egypt was failing to trust God's spoken Word for their lives. We learn of this in Hebrews 4:2: "For we also have had the gospel preached to us, just as they did; but the message they heard was of no value to them, because those who heard did not combine it with faith."

Trusting in God's Word is how faith is applied. The moment you are aware of a written promise or warning, quickly surrender your own perspective and adopt the view that God's Word prescribes. The outworking of this action occurs when you see a promise in the Scripture that is absent in your life. You should immediately seize it, claim it, and trust God for its infiltration into your life.

For example, if your children show absolutely no interest in hearing about Christ, serving Christ, or respecting your walk with Christ, claim the promise of their salvation as outlined in Acts 2:38–39. These verses capture Peter's reply to the crowd's desire for salvation:

Repent and be baptized, every one of you, in the name of Jesus Christ for the forgiveness of your sins. And you will receive the gift of the Holy Spirit. The promise is for you and your children and for all who are far off—for all whom the Lord our God will call.

This Bible passage provides grounds for you to apply your faith. You need to stand on this promise of salvation that God extends to your children. On the basis of verse 39, you can apply faith in desiring and praying this request before God. He will certainly answer you because his Word is his will. Stand on God's Word until the promise is embraced!

In order to stand on God's Word, however, you must know and understand it. At a minimum you should know how to locate a promise, even if it means scanning through the concordance at the back of your Bible for the location of a passage applicable to your need.

A candidate for church membership was asked, "What part of the Bible do you like best?"

"I like the New Testament best," he said.

Then he was asked, "What book in the New Testament is your favorite?"

He answered, "The book of the parables, sir."

He was then asked to relate one of the parables to the membership committee. And though a bit uncertain, he began . . .

Once upon a time a man went down from Jerusalem to Jericho, and fell among thieves; and the thorns grew up and choked the man. And he went on and met the Queen of

115

Sheba, and she gave that man a thousand talents of silver, and a hundred changes of raiment.

The man then got in his chariot and drove furiously, and as he was driving along under a big tree, his hair got caught in a limb and left him hanging there! He hung there many days and many nights, and the ravens brought him food to eat and water to drink.

One night while he was hanging there asleep, his wife Delilah came along and cut off his hair, and he fell on stony ground. And it began to rain, and it rained forty days and forty nights. He hid himself in a cave, and later he went on and met a man who said, "Come in and take supper with me."

But the man said, "I can't come in, for I have married a wife." And the man went out into the highways and hedges and compelled him to come in!

He then came to Jerusalem, and saw Queen Jezebel sitting high and lifted up in a window of the wall. When she saw him she laughed, and he said, "Throw her down out of there," and they threw her down. And he said, "Throw her down again," and they threw her down seventy times seven. And the fragments they picked up filled twelve baskets full! *Now*, whose wife will she be in the day of the judgment?

The membership committee agreed that this was indeed a knowledgeable candidate!

Wow! As you can see, this applicant for membership was quite confused and did not know the Scriptures. I encourage you to read and study the Bible so that you can discover God's promises for your life. Once you have secured a promise that speaks to your dilemma, stand on God's Word until that promise is fulfilled in your life.

2. Exercise Faith by Praying and Fasting

Every follower of Christ has received biblical instruction that prayer is to be a priority. Learning to follow through on that command is where both conflict and blessings lie. The early disciples asked the Master, "Lord, teach us to pray" (Luke 11:1). Apparently they knew the benefits of prayer and that it is a powerful and personal display of faith in securing answers from God. The great American evangelist Charles Finney wrote, "The Spirit leads Christians to desire and pray for things of which nothing is specifically said in the Word of God."[1] Like many other Christians down through the centuries, Finney recognized that faith is applied through prayer.

The Holy Spirit is involved in prayer. His role is to place the desire on your mind and heart to secure God's promises and provisions. As you then present your desire to the Lord in faith, he hears and answers. The prophet Jeremiah declared to God's people, "In those days when you pray, I [God] will listen. If you look for me in earnest, you will find me when you seek me" (Jer. 29:12–13 NLT). Prayer locates God. Faith secures the answer.

DOUBTING DESTROYS FAITH

Prayer should articulate faith. However, the downside of praying is the propensity to doubt. We are exhorted by the Scriptures:

> If any of you lacks wisdom, he should ask God, who gives generously to all without finding fault, and it will be given to him. But when he asks, he must believe and not doubt,

117

because he who doubts is like a wave of the sea, blown and tossed by the wind. That man should not think he will receive anything from the Lord; he is a double-minded man, unstable in all he does.

James 1:5–8

Doubt is to faith what "kryptonite" is to Superman. As this element weakens the "man of steel," doubt saps the strength of prayer by reducing it to a state of unbelief. Prayer needs faith to have an audience with God. And God, who hears our prayers asked in faith, will grant the petition. The powerful intercessor E. M. Bounds wrote:

Eminent Christians have been eminent in prayer. The deep things of God are learned nowhere else. Great things for God are done by great prayers. He who prays much, studies much, loves much, works much, does much for God and humanity. The execution of the Gospel, the vigour of faith, the maturity and excellence of spiritual graces wait on prayer.[2]

Securing great things from God is preceded by great prayers prayed in faith. Go ahead and express your faith by praying about the needs in your life. And the God of the Bible will reveal his promises in your life.

THE ROLE OF FASTING

Fasting and prayer are two separate but related spiritual activities. Prayer verbally conveys one's desire to God, while fasting physically communicates the genuine desire for answered prayer. Through abstaining from food for a

118

specific period of time, fasting communicates your earnest desire to apprehend God's promises.

The terms *fast* and *fasting* are not limited to the Christian faith or to the pages of the Bible. Throughout the ages men and women of all creeds and cultures have practiced fasting. Some exercised this discipline for political and social purposes, while others used fasting to show penance and mourning for reasons associated with their faith. The Greek philosophers Plato and Socrates, who lived in the fourth and fifth centuries before Christ, recommended fasting as an aid to mental and physical effectiveness. Mohandas Gandhi fasted as a sign of penance and as a means of political protest, believing that one could not pray without fasting or fast without praying. He described his fast as "the prayer of a soul in agony."[3]

From a biblical worldview, one of the principal reasons for fasting is for God to both see us and hear our voices on high (Isa. 58:3–4). Jesus taught that fasting is one of the disciplines of a disciple that must be practiced regularly (Matt. 6:16), like the discipline of giving (Matt. 6:2) or prayer (Matt. 6:5).

Fasting is a matter of personal choice and cannot be mandated, legislated, or used to try to manipulate God into answering you. It is a spiritual practice employed for centuries by both Old and New Testament believers to express their faith and trust in God's watchful eye. Before you launch into some extended fast, consider that fasting is like building muscle. The more you do it, the easier it becomes and the longer you can go without deciding to end the fast.

Whenever you fast, Jesus encourages you to be mindful of four things: (1) Don't behave in a pious, super-spiritual way; (2) let your facial appearance be pleasant; (3) don't broadcast the fact that you are fasting; and (4) fast in faith, expecting God to answer your request (Matt. 6:16–18). These practical guidelines always motivate me to consider the role of fasting as a means of applying faith.

Recently I found myself fasting as an expression of faith when our church was negotiating for a large parcel of land. We desperately needed a larger venue for our ministry. God had put it in my heart to build a campus—a place where our members and the local community could be served by a wide range of community services. I wanted to see athletic fields, educational buildings, senior citizen housing, dormitories, and a state-of-the-art sanctuary. The eight-month-long negotiation with the property owners "went south" a number of times. I often found myself fueling my intercession with seasons of fasting. When the day finally came to sign the contract, I gratefully attributed the victory to the power of God released through periods of fasting and prayer.

What do you want God to do for you? Whether your request is related to your family, business, or ministry, don't forget the practical and vital way to express your faith—by fasting and prayer.

3. Listen to the Holy Spirit

One of the most humbling things you can do to practically express faith is to maintain a listening attitude toward the Holy Spirit. The Holy Spirit resides in us at the point of conversion. In outlining some of the principal activities of the Holy Spirit, Jesus said:

> I have much more to say to you, more than you can now bear. But when he, the Spirit of truth, comes, he will guide you into all truth. He will not speak on his own; he will speak only what he hears, and he will tell you what is yet to come. He will bring glory to me by taking from what is mine and making it known to you. All that belongs to the Father is mine. That is why I said the Spirit will take from what is mine and make it known to you.
>
> John 16:12–15

Jesus introduces us to the ministry of the Holy Spirit by preparing us to have powerful encounters with the Spirit. These spiritual adventures are expected to usher us into understanding our inheritance as children of God. All that the Father has belongs to Jesus and will in turn be made available to us through the agency of the Holy Spirit. This is faith language to me. In other words, as we yield ourselves to the leadership and guidance of the Holy Spirit, he will bring us into the promises God has for us. But we must listen.

One reason listening is so vital is that faith is a journey with many turns and bumps in the road. I travel to the nation of Kenya every year for missionary activities. One of the vital needs in this East African country is roadwork. The roads are replete with potholes and craters, making driving quite an adventure. A trip that should take only two hours by car ends up taking four or five hours because the driver has to navigate all of the potholes in the road. Otherwise, the passengers will bump their heads on the roof of the car or the car will get a flat tire or other damage.

The journey of faith is similar. No one knows where the potholes are along the journey except the driver—the Holy Spirit. Listening to the Holy Spirit will save you a lot of unnecessary detours, stops, accidents, and flat tires (or discouragement) en route to your destination.

POSITION YOURSELF TO LISTEN

When my friend Frank accepted Jesus as his Savior, he was about six years into his marriage to Krystal. He immediately became on fire for the Lord and shared his faith zealously to Krystal every waking moment. He soon discovered that quoting Scriptures and confronting his wife were big turnoffs to her. "Stop preaching to me; I don't want to hear that stuff!" was Krystal's regular comeback. Frank wanted desperately to see Krystal experience the same kind of relationship with Jesus that he had recently found. He decided to simply pray for her salvation, thinking that her unwillingness to listen to the gospel was the real problem.

One day while in prayer, the Holy Spirit spoke to Frank's heart by illuminating a Bible promise to him: "As for me and my household, we will serve the Lord" (Josh. 24:15). This verse captured Joshua's confession that regardless of how the children of Israel chose to live, he and his family would serve God. This desire was the cry of Frank's heart. Along with sharing this promise, the Holy Spirit in a distinct way told Frank: *Stop preaching to Krystal and start living the life before her.* Dumbfounded by the wisdom and sternness in the Holy Spirit's directives, Frank decided to focus on living as an authentic Christian before his wife. His life was to become the sermon, not his words. Within eighteen months, Krystal announced, "Frank, I want what you have." Frank experienced firsthand the joy of leading his wife, Krystal, into a personal relationship with Jesus. This would not have happened if Frank had not listened to the Holy Spirit.

Learning to listen to the Holy Spirit is key. In Acts 10:9–20, we learn of a Roman centurion (an officer whose task was to oversee a hundred soldiers) named Cornelius who received an angelic visitation. Cornelius was a religious man, generous in giving monies to help those less fortunate than himself. However, he had not yet experienced salvation through Christ, which moved God to send an angel to visit him. The angelic messenger instructed Cornelius to invite Peter to his home, which in turn gave him an opportunity to hear the way to be saved. The series of events that led up to Peter's exhortation to Cornelius illustrates six distinct ways we can listen for the Holy Spirit's guidance: (1) through conviction and the witness of truth to our heart; (2) through the acknowledgment that certain activities grieve him; (3) through spiritual encounters such as dreams and visions; (4) through reflective, meditative, and prayerful times; (5) through other people's counsel and wisdom; and (6) through his distinct voice speaking a definitive word to us.

Each one of these six methods of listening to the Holy Spirit can be applied to your life today. The key is to commit to follow after the Holy Spirit and not try to take the lead.

4. Establish a Faith Confession

The words *confess* and *confession* are found in the New Testament approximately seventeen times. Our word *confess* is used to translate the Greek *homologeo*, meaning "to promise," "to agree with or consent to the desire of another," "to be in accord with someone." The popular verse used to cite the basis of confessional theology is Romans 10:9–10: "If you confess with your mouth, 'Jesus is Lord,' and believe in your heart that God raised him from the dead, you will be saved. For it is with your heart that you believe and are justified, and it is with your mouth that you confess and are saved."

Since the meaning of confession is to be in accord with someone, these verses imply that the repentant person experiences salvation because he or she is now saying the same thing that God says. *Confession of faith* brings a person into alignment and one accord with him. Confession is the acknowledgment and admission of one's newfound beliefs and perspective. The courage to reveal this new outlook requires faith in God's already stated position and perspective. In the case of salvation, your belief in and verbal admission of the revelation that Jesus is Lord seals your salvation experience.

A slightly different angle on confession is the term *faith confession*, the acknowledgment of one of God's promises outside of salvation that needs to be appropriated by faith. If the greatest gift, salvation, is confirmed and verified by confession, certainly God's other gifts and promises can be attained through similar means. When we look closer at faith confessions, we see that there are two steps in the example found in Romans 10:9–10: (1) believing in the heart and (2) confessing with the mouth.

A faith confession begins with God revealing to your heart his will regarding a promise. The moment you believe in your heart God's perspective on a matter, you are acquiescing or confessing to God that you are in complete agreement with his will about the issues at hand. Confessing is the outward acknowledgment that the inward admission outlined in the first step has already been met.

When Paul penned his letter to the Philippians, he made a faith confession by stating, "I can do everything through him who gives me strength" (4:13). Confession is not simply limited to verbal statements. Paul's faith confession occurred in writing, acknowledging that Christ gave him strength. Consequently, through this strength Paul indicated by faith to the Philippians that he could do everything. The "everything" to which Paul referred is the gospel work of Christ (Phil. 4:14–17).

If you make a public faith confession like Paul's, it must follow your private faith confession to God. In other words, before you can publicly announce or confess to anyone what you are believing God for, you must first form a private conviction of your faith claims. Unlike outward faith announcements, inward confessions keep the claims protected from external judgment of your motives or dreams. Inward, private faith confessions are vital to ensure that the focus of your faith is in alignment with God's will for your life. Since some of God's promises and our desires are personal and private, a public announcement of what we are believing God for need not take place. On the other hand, outward, public faith confessions are not necessary for God, but at times they are extremely important for other people to hear.

For example, in the case of Zacchaeus, the repentant tax collector, the townspeople needed to hear his faith confession of salvation because he had robbed them for many years. When Zacchaeus acknowledged the inward work of faith, he publicly confessed, "Look, Lord! Here and now I give half of my possessions to the poor, and if I have cheated anybody out of anything, I will pay back four times the amount" (Luke 19:8). The matter was clear to all who heard—Zacchaeus was a changed man.

On the other hand, for example, say that you are seeking God for an improved relationship in your marriage, and the Lord reveals to your heart the potential of your marriage. Your faith confession need not go public. In the privacy of your own devotions, you offer up thanksgiving and praise to God. You also privately confess back to God, "Lord, thank you for the marriage you showed me that I can have. I confess today that I will have such a marriage through your strength."

Faith confessions enable you to be in sync with God, which gives you full access to all of his promises for your life. The act of verbally conveying the truth of God's promise establishes an environment for miracles. Through faith confession you are accepting God's perspective on the matter, thus inviting him into your life to work a miracle.

5. Exercise the Power of Agreement

The words Jesus spoke on prayer comprise one of my favorite Bible passages: "Again, I tell you that if two of you on

126

earth agree about anything you ask, it will be done for you by my Father in heaven. For where two or three come together in my name, there am I with them" (Matt. 18:19–20). This passage boldly declares that answered prayer is the powerful, synergistic, and life-giving result of corporate faith—the melding together of two or more believers' faith on an agreed-upon prayer topic.

The two important words here for our study are *agree* and *together*. The word *agree* is the Greek word *symphoneo* (pronounced soom-fo-neh´-o), which means "to be harmonious," "to be in accord." It is the act of agreeing with another. The word *together* is the Greek word *synago* (pronounced soon-ag´-o), and it means "to lead," "to assemble," or "to gather together."

The word *agree* gives us a graphic word picture of a symphony playing melodious music to the audience of God. He is entertained by what he hears and sees. He's hearing the sound of faith and seeing the actions of faith. Imagine asking one or two other believers to join you in prayer. At the onset, your heart may be burdened over a specific promise of God or a need in your life that remains unfulfilled. As the subject of prayer is communicated, all the attention of the prayer partners becomes fixed on the task at hand. And in a matter of minutes, a powerful and harmonious sound of faith pierces the throne room of heaven to get God's attention. The harmony of the request powerfully expresses faith. The burden that had been lying heavily upon your heart dissipates because the power of agreement was expressed.

Has it ever occurred to you that one hundred pianos all tuned to the same tuning fork are automatically tuned to each other? They are of one accord by being tuned not to each other but to another standard to which each one must individually bow. In the same manner, two or three, or one hundred Christians for that matter, agreeing in prayer, each one looking to Christ, are in heart nearer to each other than they could possibly be by merely becoming "unity" conscious and turning their eyes away from God to strive for closer fellowship. According to A. W. Tozer, this dimension of unity can be achieved if faith is seen as a "redirecting of our vision, a getting out of the focus of our own vision and getting God into focus."[4]

The word *together* gives us a picture of the blending of strengths. Theodore E. Steinway, president of Steinway and Sons, explains that *tension* is the basis for the incredible harmony of the company's renowned concert grand pianos. This great tension, created by 243 tightly drawn strings, exerts a pull of forty thousand pounds on the iron frame of a single Steinway piano. From the perspective of the power of agreeing together in prayer, everyone's unique style and perspective become integrated, creating a synergistic experience that ushers the group into the presence of God. In fact, God declares, "There am I with them."

I remember one of the first times I incorporated this principle of the power of agreement into my arsenal of faith expressions. Our church was very small and comprised mostly of women. Now, I have nothing against women or against women as church members! But I felt that our fledgling group was unable to be a full and accurate demonstration of the life-changing power of the gospel if a limited number of men were represented in the body. So I exhorted the

128

congregation to join me the following Saturday morning at nine o'clock expressly to intercede for men to join our congregation.

About fifty of our one hundred members joined their faith with mine as we turned our Saturday morning time into a concert of prayer. At around noon, the presence of God filled the basement of the church we were renting, and we all knew that God had granted us the shared desires of all. The following Sunday, men began to pour into Christ Church—African Americans, Caucasians, Hispanics, Asians, biracial men, old men, young men, all kinds of men. Some had major emotional and financial baggage, while others brought only small "carry-ons." In either case we joyfully accepted them, knowing that God had responded to our corporate prayer of faith.

Decide today to rally a prayer troop that will assist you in applying faith toward attaining one or many of God's promises for your life. The journey of faith, accompanied by prayer, is an exciting adventure that can launch you into your destiny.

eight

⌒

Five Enemies of Faith

Two people had adjoining farms. One raised wheat and had children and large dogs. The other raised sheep. The sheep farmer was in a quandary because the dogs next door were running into his pastures and frightening the sheep. He spoke to his neighbor, but the forays continued. He thought about taking the neighbor to court. He even thought about poisoning the dogs. Then one day he found a solution.

Some new lambs were born and the sheep farmer gave each of his neighbor's children a lamb as a pet. They were delighted! Because of the pet lambs, the father could no longer let the dogs run amok. He restrained them and taught them to leave the lambs and the sheep alone . . . and everybody lived happily ever after.[1]

The sheep farmer was wise—he looked for a solution that eventually eliminated his enemy. In this case, his enemy was transformed. When it comes to faith, there are natural enemies to its expression that must be overcome and defeated. The whole idea of exercising faith is to prevail over unusual difficulties in order to appropriate God's promises into your life. Obstacles to victory must be confronted and subdued. Consequently, faith must be viewed as a weapon of warfare and not just as a nice language in which you communicate your desires to God.

A key to your developing a results-oriented level of faith is to understand that your faith is under constant attack. Sometimes the enemies to your faith are external spiritual forces; sometimes they spring from your own heart and mind. Often it is a combination of both. The forces of doubt, fear, and Satan do not give up ground without a fight. Anytime you try to advance by exercising your faith, there's always going to be some kind of demonic opposition—a counterattack, so to speak. This is why Paul instructs us in his letter to the Ephesian church that there is a combative nature to faith:

> Put on the full armor of God so that you can take your stand against the devil's schemes. For our struggle is not against flesh and blood, but against . . . the spiritual forces of evil in the heavenly realms. . . . In addition to all this, take up the shield of faith, with which you can extinguish all the flaming arrows of the evil one. Take the helmet of salvation and the sword of the Spirit, which is the word of God.
>
> Ephesians 6:11–12, 16–17

The first step in successfully fighting the good fight of faith is to know what you are fighting against. Let's examine the following five primary enemies of faith: (1) disobedience to God's Word, (2) a distorted image of God, (3) double-mindedness, (4) impatience, and (5) fear.

Disobedience to God's Word

The essence of compromise and disobedience is a decision against the life of faith. Usually disobedience to God's Word begins in a small way, then grows as a person rationalizes one act of disobedience after the next. The subsequent choice to obey or to compromise is an act either of faith or of unbelief.

The long list of actions depicting faith in Hebrews 11 can also be termed acts of obedience. Here we read that by faith Noah *warned* . . . Isaac *blessed* . . . Moses *refused* . . . Abraham *obeyed*. All of these acts and decisions of faith were also considered acts of obedience. In each instance these heroes of faith were faced with a choice of whether to take the road of obedience or disobedience. The road they chose depended on what they believed deep in their hearts.

Deliverance through Faith and Obedience

The story in Daniel 3 of the three young Hebrews who had been brought to Babylon as captives and who, against seemingly impossible odds, emerged as leaders in the nation is an outstanding example of the results of obedient faith. Shadrach, Meshach, and Abednego had been appointed as administrators over various areas of the province of Babylon. Like most people who receive promotions, they were networked with the right person. The prime minister, another Hebrew named Daniel, was their personal friend and possibly a relative.

The Assyrian kingdom, with its capital, Babylon, was located in the general area of the modern country of Iraq. Throughout the Bible, Babylon is a symbol of greed, power, and secular values, which stand in opposition to God and his kingdom. Nebuchadnezzar, king of Babylon during this period, was himself a symbol of pride and arrogance. He was so "full of himself" (as we might say today) that he commissioned an enormous, gold-plated statue of his own likeness to be erected. Then he assembled all the government workers so that with great fanfare and ceremony everyone could "freely" and dutifully bow down and worship his image. Those who did not would be cast into a blazing furnace.

As Nebuchadnezzar basked in the glory of their worship and allegiance, word came to him that the three Hebrew administrators refused to bow down. The king, unaccustomed to being refused, was enraged. He ordered that they be brought before him.

When I read this story, I wondered why they were not simply executed immediately. Perhaps the king was aware of the faithfulness the three young administrators showed toward their duties. Perhaps it was in deference to Daniel. Perhaps he thought it would make a better show if they recanted publicly. In any case, Nebuchadnezzar decided to be magnanimous and give them one more opportunity to avoid execution. If, however, they still refused to worship his image, they would be thrown into the blazing furnace. Then Nebuchadnezzar directly challenged their faith with these words: "Then what god will be able to rescue you from my hand?" (Dan. 3:15).

There was no question in the minds of the three Hebrews concerning whether God *could* deliver them. When we face situations in which we have to decide whether or not to obey God's Word, the question is never *"Can* God act on our behalf if we choose to obey?" but more often *"Will* he?" I am sure that the same question went through the minds of the three young men. The miracle they needed was unprecedented in the history of the Jews. No other individual deliverance of this magnitude had ever taken place. Having considered the matter, here is how they responded:

> O Nebuchadnezzar, we do not need to defend ourselves before you in this matter. If we are thrown into the blazing furnace, the God we serve is able to save us from it, and he will rescue us from your hand, O king. But even if he does not, we want you to know, O king, that we will not serve your gods or worship the image of gold you have set up.
>
> Daniel 3:16–18

Their determination to obey God's Word so enraged the king that he ordered the furnace heated seven times hotter. I'm not sure what his intention was. The hotter furnaces would only serve to put them out of their misery more quickly, but despots typically do irrational things when people choose to obey a higher law. The superheated furnace only served to kill the king's servants when they drew near enough to cast the three Hebrews into the oven.

The whole event was designed to publicly teach a lesson to those who dared disobey the king. It taught a lesson all right, but certainly not the one Nebuchadnezzar had planned. The young men were tied up and thrown into the fire with all their clothes on. Suddenly, the king leaped to his feet in amazement and asked his advisers, "Weren't there three men that we tied up and threw into the fire? . . . Look! I see four men walking around in the fire, unbound and unharmed, and the fourth looks like a son of the gods" (Dan. 3:24–25).

When Shadrach, Meshach, and Abednego came out of the fire, the whole assembly saw that the fire had no effect on them. Their clothes didn't even hold the smell of smoke. The astounded king then ordered everyone to worship the God of the Hebrews. And in keeping with his way of getting things done, he ordered that anyone who refused be torn limb from limb. That's not exactly God's recommended method of evangelism, but it does reveal that the young men's faith and obedience made quite an impression on Nebuchadnezzar. In the end, they were all promoted.

Two Ways, One Decision

There are several lessons in this story: that God will be with us in the fires of life; that God can use simple faith and obedience to touch the hardest of hearts; that regardless of whether or not we are delivered, obedience to God is not negotiable.

The point here is that *disobedience is an enemy of faith.* God allows us into situations in which we simply have to trust him. Sometimes it is for a public display of God's power. Sometimes it is to touch the lives of others. Sometimes the purpose is simply to grow our faith. Often it is all of the above.

In many of these situations, however, we are presented a "way of escape" through disobedience to God's Word. Shadrach, Meshach, and Abednego could have escaped danger by bowing to the statue. But they chose to obey whether God chose to deliver them or not. I do not want to be misunderstood here. Though God heals, delivers, and provides, I am *not* suggesting that it is wrong to go to the doctor, buy insurance, or save money for the future. Applying our faith always includes a combination of God's part and our part. Disobedience becomes an enemy of faith when we directly disobey God's Word rather than trusting in him. For example, we can trust God to meet a particular need or we can attempt to meet the need ourselves by cheating on our tax return to get the money. Choosing to cheat is a decision against the life of faith.

Disobedience comes in the form of options. These options at times appear innocent, but if heeded, they render faith impotent. In the case of the Hebrew men, they had the option of worshiping the king's statue or being thrown into the fiery furnace. Choosing the furnace was the action of obedience in this instance. The young men were being obedient to the first and second commandments: "You shall have no other gods before me" and "You shall not make for yourself an idol in the form of anything in heaven above or on the earth beneath or in the waters below. You shall not bow down to them or worship them; for I, the LORD your God, am a jealous God" (Exod. 20:3–4).

Consider your present trial. Are you flirting with disobedience? Are there shortcuts that look tempting? Keep in mind that your faith—and the exercise of that faith—is more precious than gold, which perishes. Compromising obedience means that you'll have to "repeat the class" of faith later. It may not be the same trial on the next go-round, but it will be the same issue of faith that you must face and conquer.

Disobedience to God's Word is an enemy to faith. Defeat it and grow in the Lord.

A Distorted Image of God

Do you see God the way he wants you to see him?

Many years ago I decided to try out a new barbershop. The first time I walked into the shop, four barbers were busy cutting hair and there were about ten guys ahead of me. I took a seat and waited for about twenty minutes. Eventually one of the barbers, who happened to be extremely cross-eyed, finished with his client, turned in my general direction, and said, "You're next." I knew it was my turn, but he was looking one way and pointing another—and neither was exactly toward me.

"Come on, you're next," he urged impatiently.

"Me?" I asked, checking out his line of sight and the direction he was pointing. Neither was close to where I was seated.

"Yeah, you," he retorted. "Are you blind?"

No, but I was a little confused and thrown off balance by the fact that the barber had a different way of looking at things. Just because someone is convinced about their version of reality, and just because they are in charge, doesn't mean they are right. And it doesn't mean I have to see things their way. The world around us has a tremendous influence on our ideas. Often believers absorb the world's varied and sometimes distorted images of God, and this distortion becomes an enemy to faith.

Who Shapes Your View of God?

What is your image of God, and who shapes that image? Don't let politicians, broadcasters, reporters, or celebrities become your theologians. Not only will they give you the wrong answers, they will ask the wrong questions. Nebuchadnezzar stated, in essence, that he possessed the final authority over the lives of the three young Hebrews and asked, "What god will be able to rescue you from my hand?"

They might have thought to themselves, *Hmm . . . you know, that's a good question.* Not only had *they* been delivered into the king's hands, so had their homeland, the nation of Judah. Nebuchadnezzar had leveled Jerusalem, plundered the temple, and taken the people into captivity. To the casual bystander it didn't seem that the God of Abraham, Isaac, and Jacob was much of a match for the Babylonian king.

Maybe you have heard questions like these from the mouths of others or maybe you've contemplated them yourself:

If God really loves me, how could he allow this to happen?

If God is loving and powerful, why is there evil in the world?

If God is all-powerful, why doesn't he just prevent evil and make all people good?

I thought you said God was going to help you get a job. Wouldn't you have been better off if you hadn't decided to follow Jesus?

Where do you think those voices come from? Regardless of their immediate source, ultimately they are from Satan. It was Satan who tempted Eve in the garden by distorting her understanding of God, saying, "You will not surely die [if you eat the fruit from the forbidden tree]. . . . For God knows that when you eat of it your eyes will be opened, and you will be like God, knowing good and evil" (Gen. 3:4). There was some truth in what Satan said. But the sum of what he said was a big lie. The subtle implication was that God's command was issued out of some selfish and sinister motive. Satan seemed to be saying, "God is just trying to keep you down, to hold you back from achieving your potential."

The enemy of faith seeks to distort our image of God. Often the distortion comes not in the form of a direct accusation but as a question that changes the context of the way we see God. Notice again how Shadrach, Meshach, and Abednego responded to the king's question:

O Nebuchadnezzar, we do not need to defend ourselves before you in this matter. If we are thrown into the blazing furnace, the God we serve is able to save us from it, and he will rescue us from your hand, O king. But even if he does not, we want you to know, O king, that we will not serve your gods or worship the image of gold you have set up.

Daniel 3:16–18

The three young Hebrews refused to let the king define the terms of their faith in or allegiance to God. This is an excellent lesson, one that needs to be preached in every church in America. Another significant truth expressed in this account is this: Just because you obey God and follow his commands doesn't mean that God is obligated to deliver you from every terrible ordeal. Most people accept this reality of God's sovereignty or his independence and self-governing ability. The problem is that they just don't like it, which means they struggle in future dealings with God by holding a grudge against his church or his laws.

A Culturally Defined God?

Throughout history the church has been tempted to define God in terms of the current economic, cultural, and political norms. In medieval times, certain assumptions about God were allowed to grow out of the concept of the divine right of kings. In other words, people tend to interface with God as they would an earthly person, especially a king. And people tend to draw from their social experiences and societal structures a set of principles through which they filter their theology, belief systems, and expectations. A highly class-conscious culture led many to assume that God approved of "the way things were" with regard to literacy, economics, and social status. All of this affected the way people understood God.

In medieval times, ordinary people didn't get a chance to interpret the Bible or really think for themselves. Social structures were imposed on them by those in power. Compare these ideas with those in modern America, the most democratic, most technologically advanced, and richest nation in history. Those factors also tend to shape how we see and understand God. Many of us here in the United States think of God as an American, just as people in previous times thought of him as British nobility, a Roman Catholic bishop, or the notable Jewish Pharisee. These thoughts are not necessarily verbalized, but they are present to the point at which our perspectives of God and the world around us are colored by them.

Today the church of Jesus Christ is primarily non-Western, nonwhite people who live in developing nations ruled by nondemocratic governments. Americans should be reminded that God is much bigger than the United States of America. The problem is that we all like to think that God is just like us. We visualize him in our own image. In fact, every culture at every point in history has faced stumbling blocks that threatened to distort their image of God, and with it, their faith.

Sometimes I get the impression that we Americans think that when we get to heaven we are going to see the throne of God draped with the Stars and Stripes. But God is not an American, nor is his agenda strictly an American agenda. If we don't see past our own cultural perspective, we run the risk of developing a distorted image of God. People who live in the greatest consumer society that has ever existed tend to develop a theology in which they assume that God approves of our defining every whim as a need, every inconvenience an injustice, and every trial a tragedy. We need to let our minds and our faith be influenced by God's Word, not pop-culture theology.

That is precisely what was going on in the dialogue between Nebuchadnezzar and the young Hebrews. However, they refused to let the king's distorted understanding of God and the power of Babylon pollute their theology or their determination to stand in faith.

Double-Mindedness

One of the greatest difficulties people have in trusting God is in becoming clear about what they are trusting God for. They waver about precisely what they need or should be praying for. This indecisiveness, which James calls being "double-minded," is an enemy of faith. James puts it like this:

> If any of you lacks wisdom, he should ask God, who gives generously to all without finding fault, and it will be given to him. But when he asks, he must believe and not doubt, because he who doubts is like a wave of the sea, blown and tossed by the wind. That man should not think he will receive anything from the Lord; he is a double-minded man, unstable in all he does.
>
> James 1:5–8

Have you ever met a person who was double-minded about trusting God? One day he is down; the next day he is up. One day he is sure that God can and will answer his prayer; the next day he's in despair about God acting on his behalf. One day he has a God-given calling; the next day he is convinced he should be following other pursuits.

I am not referring to the ups and downs of the fight of faith. I'm just like the next guy. I fight my way through doubts and fears while trying to take that hill by faith. And when the devil launches an artillery barrage and takes back the ground, I counterattack, with all my friends praying for me. Back and forth it goes until I receive the promise by faith and patience. If struggling with questions and fears disqualifies a person, I would have been out of this fight long ago! In my opinion, James is talking here not about the struggle of standing in faith for what you believe but about constantly changing what you believe.

Generally speaking, if you believe that God exists on Tuesday, but on Thursday you feel that you're all alone in your fight, you should not expect any great miracles. The same is true for personal prayer and specific requests. If one week you are trusting God to solidify you in the company through a promotion, but the following week you're asking him to open a position for you with your company's chief competitor, you are double-minded.

The Wisdom of Being Sure of What We Want

When you find yourself lacking clarity about what you are asking and trusting God for, James says to ask for wisdom. The wisdom you receive will help you clarify your emotions and your perspective of the need (or trial). It will also enable you to develop a workable strategy for moving forward, even if nothing changes.

We have seen how faith is defined in Hebrews 11:1: "Now faith is being sure of what we hope for and certain of what we do not see." If you think of faith in terms of that definition, you can see how double-mindedness is your enemy. Faith is an inner resolve or conclusion about a matter. Since faith means "being sure," then being unsure or fickle erodes the infrastructure of your faith.

An American campus minister serving in Australia gave a testimony that illustrates this point. The airfare for a family of four to travel back to the United States for Christmas was expensive, so they did not always make the trip. Several months after another painful holiday season away from their extended family, the husband put his faith in God that the airfare would be provided for the following Christmas. He announced to his children that they would spend the next Christmas with their grandparents in the States. Although his wife wasn't too sure about what her husband had done, the kids immediately set their hearts on the trip. His response was, "I cannot be wishy-washy about this. I have to either believe God or not."

Speaking in an American church the following December, he said in regard to this and several other similar experiences that faith begins when we "lock in" to what we are requesting from God. That doesn't mean we should try to "tempt God" by threatening to walk away if he does not come through. It doesn't mean we should create a crisis

145

trying to force God's hand. It does mean that faith requires confidence and inner resolve. The result of that kind of faith is inner assurance. In other words, faith needs a clear target, a goal not just to aim for at the moment but to keep in our sights.

Developing your faith about a particular matter involves seeking God's guidance and making a decision to become resolute on your stance about the issue. You have to seek wisdom, get clarity, and then come to a resolution.

Believing God for his promises is an extension of seeking God for his will. Sometimes, to defeat our double-mindedness, we need to go away and pray. Dr. Billy Graham gives the personal account of one of his struggles with double-mindedness:

In August of 1949, I was so filled with doubts about everything that when I stood to preach and made a statement, I would say to myself: I wonder if that is the truth. I wonder if I can really say that sincerely. My ministry had gone. I then took the Bible up into the high Sierra Nevada mountains in California. I opened it and got on my knees. I pled, "Father I cannot understand many things in this Book. I cannot come intellectually all the way, but I accept it by faith to be authoritative, the inspired Word of the living God!"[2]

Alone with God, Dr. Graham received clarity and resolve about his faith. Within the next two years, he was catapulted to national prominence.

Impatience

We are exhorted in Hebrews 6:12 to "imitate those who through faith and patience inherit what has been promised." The speed with which your prayers are answered is not necessarily a function of how much faith you have. God has his own timing, and he doesn't hurry or delay. Consequently, impatience becomes one of the enemies of our faith. If your faith is not married to patience, then you run the risk of missing God's promise.

Scripture points to Abraham as the great example of hoping against all hope, of trusting in God's promise to make from his descendants a great nation, even though he and Sarah were advanced in age. Their biological clocks had ticked out.

Though Abraham's faith was reckoned to him as righteousness, that doesn't mean he didn't have to fight with impatience. In fact, he even lost a few battles. Having grown weary of waiting for the promised child through Sarah, Abraham allowed her to persuade him to sleep with Hagar, Sarah's maidservant, in order to have a child. Ishmael, the child of Abraham and Hagar, became the father of the Arabs. Eventually Sarah did miraculously become pregnant and gave birth to Isaac, the promised child from whom the Jews are descended. However, because Abraham's impatience led to a bad choice, things didn't go well at home. And the descendants of Hagar and Sarah have been fighting ever since.

Many of us have created some metaphorical "Ishmaels" that have come back to haunt us simply because we gave in to impatience. Because of our impatience, we try to replicate

God's promise in our own way and by our own strength. Can God redeem and use those situations? Certainly he can and he will.

The point is that our impatience often causes us to have to settle for second best. That is particularly true in relationships. "I can't wait; my biological clock is ticking," a woman who wants to marry may say. So she accepts the first proposal that comes along, and the relationship often doesn't blossom as well as if she had waited. If you compromise and settle for second best, it is because you prefer your own plans over God's plan, for which you have to wait. As you can see, choices are about faith and patience.

Our church has been looking for seven years for a piece of property in the northern New Jersey region that lends itself to a campus setting. We have outgrown our present sanctuary. As a result, we have five Sunday morning services. When a 107-acre site was brought to our attention, I negotiated a deal as quickly as possible. The cost was a bargain, considering the premiums placed on property in our area. Although the move will prove to be an expensive one born out of faith, our congregation learned to be patient for the manifestation of the property. It was incredibly tempting to quickly accept other property opportunities, even when we knew deep down they were not God's choice. Impatience is a formidable enemy of faith. But patience is a great friend of faith.

Impatience often keeps us from learning valuable lessons that are available only to those who have to wait to receive God's promise in God's timing. Recently I came across one of my old prayer journals. I started journaling years ago simply

148

by making prayer lists in a book to review in my time of prayer and study. I marveled as I read through the old journal, not just at what God had done over time but at the things for which I asked and how I prioritized my requests. Almost every page of that particular journal revealed the smallness of my perspective and shortsightedness of my prayer. I began to give sincere thanks to God for the prayers I had listed that he, in his wisdom, did *not* answer.

Faith and patience in God's promises are often related to God's calling. We want God to use us, to raise us up in our ministries, to promote us in our careers, and to demonstrate his power by how quickly he can do so.

Researchers at the University of Chicago once analyzed the careers of concert pianists, artists, and athletes to determine what process led to success. Regarding concert pianists, the research revealed that the musicians worked an average of 17.1 years from the day they began taking piano lessons until the day they won a major competition.[3] That takes patience and persistence—the same things we must add to faith to inherit the promises of God.

The Paralysis of Fear

Stepping out in faith always involves risk. The greater the step of faith, the greater the risk involved. The greater the gift we hope to gain from God, the greater the loss of self-defined goals we may experience. It is easy, then, to see how an intense fear of loss can paralyze a person's faith.

Sometimes challenges to faith come upon us like a storm at sea. Other times they are the result of our own decisions.

Either way, we almost invariably encounter obstacles on the way to our chosen life destination. In such cases, the easiest way to avoid the risk is to turn back from our purpose and pursue a less-challenging calling.

That was the situation with those to whom the book of Hebrews was written (cf. 5:11). These Jewish Christians were tempted to go back, to backslide from following Christ, because there was much less risk involved in simply being "old covenant" Jews. Remember, compromise and disobedience begin in a decision against the life of faith. To show the value of faith, Hebrews says it was "by faith" that the men of old gained approval in their choices and actions (11:2). Though faith is compared to a small mustard seed, its value is great in size, similar to that of a mountain.

Perhaps the greatest enemy of faith is the fear of what may be lost. This little exercise will illustrate what I mean. On the left, below, list the three biggest challenges to your faith—the things you have the hardest time trusting God about with an inner confidence and assurance. Then, in the right-hand column, write down what you stand to lose.

Challenge to Faith		Risk Involved
1. _____	→	_____
2. _____	→	_____
3. _____	→	_____

Analyze the risk, or what you are afraid of losing or not gaining. If you can come to terms with that, then faith becomes a lot easier. Isn't that precisely what happened with

Shadrach, Meshach, and Abednego? "He will rescue us from your hand," they said to Nebuchadnezzar. "But even if he does not, we want you to know, O king, that we will not serve your gods or worship the image of gold you have set up" (Dan. 3:17–18). Fear is a natural response. However, in this instance, fear did not rule them. Consequently, their faith and dedication prevailed.

The Security of Dying to Self

One of the keys to having unshakable, fully assured faith is dying to our own desires. To the Colossian church Paul wrote, "For you died, and your life is now hidden with Christ in God" (Col. 3:3). And to the Philippians, "For to me, to live is Christ and to die is gain" (Phil. 1:21).

Having a struggle with faith? We all do at times; some of us, a lot of the time. God allows us into those situations because that is how our faith grows. But the real issue may be the fact that we are clinging to, grasping, and loving the things of this life—including our own desires. Some so covet this world that it has become an enemy of their faith. For this reason, noted author and pastor Jim Cymbala writes, "The great battle of our spiritual lives is 'Will you believe?' It is not 'Will you try harder?' or 'Can you make yourself worthy?' It is squarely a matter of believing that God will do what only he can do. That is what God honors."[4]

What more can I say other than amen! Let nothing hinder you, not even the challenges of dying to self, from achieving God's destiny for your life. Press on by faith and lay hold of his plan for your life and family.

nine

~~~

FAITH DOES NOT STAND ALONE

A man had been shipwrecked on a deserted island, far from the traditional shipping lanes and thousands of miles from other inhabited islands. He lived in that remote place for many years and learned to live apart from any other human contact or companionship. Eventually a ship passed by the island, and the old castaway was able to send up a signal. The ship's captain came ashore to see how this man had survived for all those years. Noticing three well-constructed huts, the captain asked the man to explain their use.

"The first hut is my house," said the sole resident of the island, "and the second hut is my church."

"And the third?" the captain inquired.

"Well," said the old man. "That's a sad story. The third hut is the church I used to attend."

This story illustrates how fickle people can be. They quit their jobs, divorce their spouses, and leave their churches. When you dig down and discover what caused them to abandon these relationships, the reasons are often relatively trivial. I have even heard some say, "I just felt like it." In many cases they simply got tired of the relationship; they didn't feel it was doing as much for them as it used to, so they just left. It doesn't matter what kind of relationship it is—business, friendship, romantic, or spiritual—if you are only in it for yourself, the relationship will be short-lived or shallow.

Faith and the Church

You can attend all the seminars, read all the books, and go to endless counseling sessions, but without a sense of shared purpose and vision, relationships have no power. Periodically we need to stop, take a look at all our activities and involvements, and then ask ourselves a fundamental question: What is our purpose here?

What we Christians do as a matter of habit more than anything else is attend church. And why? The answer should be: (1) to establish relationships with other believers and (2) because we agree with the mission of the church. Unfortunately, most people make decisions about church membership based on the performance of the musicians or the style of the speaker. I have even known of people choosing to become members of a church because the church had no financial needs! They were tired of being asked to support the work of other churches financially. Without an overriding sense of purpose and vision, parishioners can easily begin to view themselves as consumers. Unwittingly they see the pastor as a performer and the church board as advertisers of the organization's products and services—serving only to increase their market share among potential churchgoers. This is a primary reason people are so fickle and flighty about their church commitment.

The Bible teaches that God loves each individual and has a plan for his or her life. On the other hand, the Bible also teaches that God has a corporate plan for his people, the church. Independent, individualistic Americans are not so quick to embrace such an idea. We tend to think of faith and purpose in terms of the "what's in it for me?" consumer model. But the Scriptures show that the great examples and admonitions about faith and unbelief usually relate to corporate faith. Abraham, Sarah, Moses, David, Paul, and others are great examples of faith, but their faith was expressed primarily for God's purposes to be accomplished for and through his people. In contrast, examples of unbelief are people who fixated on their own needs, goals, and desires rather than the purpose of God through his covenant people (first Israel, then the church).

One of my objectives in this book has been to give you a balanced view of faith. Authentic biblical faith focuses on God's purpose for the church, the community, the nation, and the world. Obviously such a broad impact requires a corporate effort. Think about it. Every great example and admonition about faith in the New Testament has to do with people endeavoring to become more effective witnesses for Christ or to be of greater service to his church. Faith was focused on God's purpose.

Nothing is wrong with praying for the things we need personally and coming to Christ with the things that burden our own hearts. However, if the object of your prayers and the goals of your faith are completely dominated by your own personal desires, hopes, and dreams, then you have a distorted understanding of faith. If you really want to develop authentic biblical faith, you need a bigger vision. You must begin to stand in faith for God's purposes through the church for your *generation*, not just for your own life.

Stirring Up the Corporate Faith

One of the best Old Testament case studies about corporate faith is found in Numbers 13. The pharaoh of Egypt was persuaded by a series of extraordinary plagues to allow the Hebrew nation of slaves to simply walk away from their captivity. Under the leadership of Moses, they made their way across the Red Sea and the wilderness. As they drew near to the Promised Land of Canaan, the Lord instructed Moses to "send some men to explore the land of Canaan, which I am giving to the Israelites. From each ancestral tribe send one of its leaders" (Num. 13:1–2). Moses followed God's orders and sent out the spies on a reconnaissance mission, instructing them to gather data about the people, the land, and the land's defenses.

Defeating the Canaanites would be no easy task; they were a very large and intimidating people. However, the land was inhabited by about a dozen different groups with no strong alliance to one another. They were people already ripe for God's judgment (Gen. 15:16). The Canaanites were no challenge compared to the might of Egypt, the most powerful nation on earth at that time. Yet God had taken care of Pharaoh, and all the Hebrews had to do was pack up and leave. You would think that the children of Israel could simply walk into Canaan in the wake of a few earth-shaking miracles, announce that they were there to take possession of the land, and give the bad guys twenty-four hours to get out of town.

But unlike the exodus from Egypt, it didn't happen that way. At the border of Canaan the Israelites were sending out spies, drawing up battle plans, sharpening swords, and whatever else people did back then to get ready for war. The exodus from Egypt seemed so spiritual, but this seemed so practical.

In our daily walk with the Lord, we need to be careful not to overspiritualize situations. Working hard on matters that contribute to our objectives is not abdicating faith. What Moses did in sending out the spies was by God's instruction. The lesson we need to learn from this is that there are times and seasons in which faith means simply standing still and waiting for God to move in his timing. Then there are other times when faith means stepping out to work hard in practical ways. For most of the challenges in our lives, victory will require a combination of God doing his part and us doing our part.

Enrolling People in the Organization

Take a look at the instructions Moses gave to the twelve spies:

"Go up through the Negev and on into the hill country. See what the land is like and whether the people who live there are strong or weak, few or many. What kind of land do they live in? Is it good or bad? What kind of towns do they live in? Are they unwalled or fortified? How is the soil? Is it fertile or poor? Are there trees on it or not? Do your best to bring back some of the fruit of the land." (It was the season for the first ripe grapes.)

Numbers 13:17–20

Here we find a wonderful illustration of a group of people called to do something *together* that required great faith.

God instructed Moses to recruit scouts from every tribe. One of the benefits of this strategy is that every segment of the organization would share ownership in the mission. Every great leader knows that he or she has to give those who follow him or her a clear vision. For people to join together in faith and establish a coordinated effort to accomplish great things, they all have to see the vision clearly.

Just imagine parading that cluster of grapes through the various tribes. That is not unlike putting a picture on your refrigerator to illustrate your faith goals. The idea is that you have clearly visualized the object of your faith and helped others see it as well.

If you ask typical church people to explain the corporate mission and faith objectives of their church, you might get some strange, bewildered looks. Many answers would be something like this: construct a new building, pay for a new building, renovate an old building, get new hymnbooks, purchase a new organ, find a new preacher, and so on. Yet none of these activities represents the mission of the church. Staff and facilities are only means to an end. The mission of the church has to be more than maintaining itself.

In this story, Moses was the vision keeper, the one to whom God entrusted the plan for his people. People who walk in a faith that is fully assured and resolute are those who see things not merely as they are (Rom. 4:17). One of the characteristics of great leaders is that they are able to see where the organization is going and what it will look like when they get there.

In fact, faith-filled visionaries sometimes see the future with such clarity that they have trouble distinguishing between future vision and present reality. That tendency drives management and accounting types crazy because they tend to focus on the practical realities of the present. Obviously we need both kinds of people in the church. Visionary leadership is important because it clarifies the mission of the church and challenges the faith of every member.

Unbelief, Exaggeration, and "Awfulizing"

After forty days, the twelve spies returned and reported to Moses and all the people:

We went into the land to which you sent us, and it does flow with milk and honey! Here is its fruit. But the people who live there are powerful, and the cities are fortified and very large. We even saw descendants of Anak there. The Amalekites live in the Negev; the Hittites, Jebusites and

Amorites live in the hill country; and the Canaanites live
near the sea and along the Jordan.

Numbers 13:27–29

Everyone loved the part about the flowing milk and honey.
And the grapes! The fruit was like nothing they had ever
seen. But when they heard about the fortified cities, they
began to have second thoughts.

It is unclear exactly who Anak was, but the presence
of his descendants did not seem to be a welcome thought
because they were "strong and tall" (Deut. 9:2). The chorus
of those wanting to express their doubts about the mission
grew louder and louder until finally one of the spies, Caleb,
silenced them and said, "'We should go up and take possession of the land, for we can certainly do it.' But the men who
had gone up with him said, 'We can't attack those people;
they are stronger than we are'" (Num. 13:30–31).

Apparently the meeting broke up at that point, and everyone went back to his or her own camp. The next thing
we read about is what the ten doubting spies began to do.

And they spread among the Israelites a bad report about the
land they had explored. They said, "The land we explored
devours those living in it. All the people we saw there are of
great size. We saw the Nephilim there (the descendants of
Anak come from the Nephilim). We seemed like grasshoppers in our own eyes, and we looked the same to them."

Numbers 13:32–33

Have you ever noticed that, like misery, doubt and unbelief love company? Those who have abandoned faith can

160

hardly resist trying to convert others to their position. You also may have noticed that when people begin to give a "bad report," every time the story is told the news becomes grimmer and grimmer. The land flowing with milk and honey in the spies' first report had gradually turned into the land that "devours those living in it."

And concerning the people who were described as "large," before long they had become hundreds of times *larger*, so that the Israelites by comparison were "like grasshoppers." The naysayers were fully engaged in what we may call "awfulizing," and the longer they were allowed to talk, the more awful the situation appeared. It even progressed to the point at which the people became convinced of the foolishness of their mission.

God had already established that he was going to give the land of Canaan to the Israelites. However, the ten spies misunderstood their assignment. They were sent to find out *how* they could take the land, not *if* they could take it. Looking at a problem or an objective from a not-*if*-but-*how* perspective makes all the difference in the world. That is why it is so important for a congregation of believers to understand what God has called them to be and do. Without a sense of divine purpose and calling, every objective requiring a significant step of faith causes people to start questioning the mission rather than asking God for his wisdom and strategy.

The unbelief of the ten spies spread and eventually poisoned the corporate faith of the whole camp of Israel. Much later Jesus would say to the Pharisees, "You brood of vipers, how can you who are evil say anything good? For out of the overflow of the heart the mouth speaks" (Matt. 12:34).

161

Whatever is in our hearts tends to come out of our mouth. Consequently, without even realizing it, we can either encourage or discourage other people's faith.

Just as fear and unbelief spread rapidly through the camp of Israel, so many "believing congregations" can include a group of nonbelievers—those who either do not believe in the corporate vision or perhaps even doubt the fundamentals of the Christian faith. A small group of people within a large congregation usually does not have a significant effect on the mission of the church. However, when confronted with obstacles and challenges to their faith, the doubters begin to step forward onto center stage.

"Aha!" we hear. "We told you this would not work. This project was destined to fail. See, we were right all along. You should have listened to us. . . ."

The I-told-you-so's are usually followed by more awfulizing: "We're going to fail! We're going to lose everything! We'll become the laughingstock of the community! It will ruin the church. It's going to be simply awful!"

In Israel's case, the small group of doubters was eventually able to persuade the larger body of the children of Israel. You don't have to convert everyone in an organization to change its character. When a sufficient number of people buy into a belief or disbelief, you reach a kind of critical mass. That idea then becomes the group's dominant worldview. When that point was reached in Israel, all those who were wavering between faith and doubt almost immediately joined the doubters—the awfulizers.

Typically that middle group, which is susceptible to wavering, represents the majority of a family, community, church,

162

or other organization. With their capitulation to doubt, the children of Israel as a whole became an "unbelieving congregation," containing only a small group of those who continued to trust God. Notice the change that took place and what happened to the corporate vision for the Promised Land:

> That night all the people of the community raised their voices and wept aloud. All the Israelites grumbled against Moses and Aaron, and the whole assembly said to them, "If only we had died in Egypt! Or in this desert! Why is the LORD bringing us to this land only to let us fall by the sword? Our wives and children will be taken as plunder. Wouldn't it be better for us to go back to Egypt?" And they said to each other, "We should choose a leader and go back to Egypt."
> Numbers 14:1–4

Listen to these people. All together they were weeping and grumbling against the leaders. The children of Israel weren't just rejecting the mission; they were rejecting the faith altogether. They were convinced that God was plotting to kill them. They wished they were either dead or still slaves in Egypt. Then someone came up with an idea. "Hey, maybe we can go back to Egypt and be slaves again!" I hate to say it, but I know of some church situations that sound a lot like this.

Moses and his leadership team were in a difficult spot. God had given them the land as surely as he had delivered them from Egypt. They were fully assured in their faith and they could see it. But the people did not. Moses and Aaron gathered the people and tried to reassure them. Joshua and Caleb, the two spies who believed, also tried to stir up the people's faith:

"If the LORD is pleased with us," they said, "he will lead us into that land, a land flowing with milk and honey, and will give it to us. Only do not rebel against the LORD. And do not be afraid of the people of the land, because we will swallow them up. Their protection is gone, but the LORD is with us. Do not be afraid of them."

Numbers 14:8–9

Once the power of fear and doubt gains momentum, it's difficult to stop it. Joshua and Caleb did their best, but it was like standing in front of a runaway train. The doubters refused to be encouraged, and they did not appreciate Moses and his team persisting with the vision. They immediately began to discuss stoning the leaders.

As church leaders and as church members, we have to decide right up front what kind of church we want to build or join. If we want to be part of a church dedicated to a clearly defined mission, then people must embrace the calling of God on the church and stand in faith together to see it accomplished. If we simply want to be Sunday morning spectators, then there are plenty of places where we can do that. But the concern of this chapter and this book is the development of our faith. If we want to grow in faith, we must join with a group of people where our faith can be exercised on something bigger than ourselves and our own interests.

The Challenge to Leadership

Just about the time the stoning proposal was about to be acted upon, the Lord demonstrated his disapproval:

But the whole assembly talked about stoning them. Then the glory of the LORD appeared at the Tent of Meeting to all the Israelites. The LORD said to Moses, "How long will these people treat me with contempt? How long will they refuse to believe in me, in spite of all the miraculous signs I have performed among them? I will strike them down with a plague and destroy them, but I will make you [Moses] into a nation greater and stronger than they."

Numbers 14:10–12

Now here is a challenge to leadership, especially church leadership. Imagine yourself a pastor who felt called to a particular church body. After a few years, however, that congregation decided that the walk of faith was a little too risky. The harder you tried to stir their faith, the more resistant they became. One day during a glorious prayer time, an idea pops into your head. Take the committed, faithful members, move across town, and start a new church. Then you could really do something great for the Lord.

It's hard to say what the Lord would think about that. Every situation is different, and the suggestion to Moses to separate the faithful from the doubters came from the Lord himself. But Moses's response was to intercede for the majority of the children of Israel, not for their sakes but for the sake of the glory of God. He argued with God that if God rejected his people, it would not bring glory to the Lord's name. "If you put these people to death all at one time," Moses prayed, "the nations who have heard

165

this report about you will say, 'The LORD was not able to bring these people into the land he promised them on oath; so he slaughtered them in the desert'" (Num. 14:15–16). Despite Moses's intercession, at the end of the trial only Joshua and Caleb, who had returned with a good report and stood in faith with Moses and Aaron, lived to enter the Promised Land with the next generation of Israelites.

Of all the examples of faith in Hebrews 11, almost a fourth of the chapter is devoted to Abraham and Moses. There is a great lesson on faith regarding the way Moses responded to God's proposition. He could have used his faith to build his own name, his own family, and his own kingdom. Had Moses accepted the offer, to this day the Jews would have been known as the children of Moses rather than the children of Israel. Instead Moses continued to exercise his faith on what would demonstrate God's glory and purpose for the larger congregation of Israel. In other words, faith, as exemplified by Moses, is not simply faith for our own needs and wants but faith for God's larger plan and purpose.

Inspiring Corporate Faith

The doubts about God's faithfulness, the evil reports, and the awfulizing undermined the faith of the congregation. That generation never envisioned what God had promised, let alone attained it. I suspect that those responsible never set out to oppose the God of Abraham, Isaac, and Jacob. However, by simply giving in to their fears, that is exactly what they wound up doing.

Conversely, giving in to faith can cause powerful visions and dreams to be realized by the church or group of which you are a part. When our congregation was eight years old, we finally discovered a building that was available that could seat approximately a thousand people. Eight years was a long time, and I had looked high and low for a permanent home for our rapidly growing congregation, to no avail. Given the cost and scarcity of buildings zoned for a church in the northern New Jersey market, the task was a daunting one. But the day came when a building located ten minutes from our present rental hall was placed on the market for $1,250,000. After five minutes of touring the structure, though the property was dilapidated and worn, I said to the realtor, "We'll take it." He quickly furnished a sales agreement, which I quickly signed. Then he immediately notified me that I needed $100,000 by Monday as the down payment to solidify the deal. It was Friday, and my congregation had only a few dollars in the bank.

That Friday and Saturday I sought the Lord like never before. I thought to myself, *I don't have $100,000, and if I did, I would pay the down payment out of my own savings.* After several hours of crying out to God in prayer, the Holy Spirit spoke to my heart and said, "David, just ask the congregation for the money. Ask for people to give different-size gifts until they total $100,000." Have you ever noticed that when the Holy Spirit speaks, it makes so much sense that you sit there speechless for a few minutes? Such was the case that Saturday morning. After that moment, I made a few telephone calls to some of our leaders requesting that they use the telephone chain and alert every member that the next day I would be sharing some exciting news that they would not want to miss. At that time, our congregation was approximately five hundred members.

That Saturday night, I wrestled as I slept because of all the anxiety I felt about Sunday. If I did not receive $100,000 cash by the end of Sunday worship, the sale agreement would be voided and another congregation would likely purchase the property. The morning came and I quickly got the family ready for church. Our usual liturgy begins with worship and singing followed by a pastoral greeting. Because the members had received a mysterious telephone call the day before, everyone was teeming with excitement and could hardly wait for me to share the good news.

Recognizing the time had come, I asked the ushers to distribute a photograph of the new facility to each congregant. On Friday I had had a photographer take a picture from the balcony of the large stained-glass window located behind the altar. I wanted everyone to get a perspective of the opportunity God had placed before us. When they saw the photo of what I described as our future home, the place erupted with shouts. After ten minutes, I calmed everyone down with this announcement: "Folks, there is only one issue. Before I leave through those double doors [pointing to the exit doors], I need to receive $100,000 cash from you." The place instantly became quiet. You could hear a pin drop. Some people tore up their picture while muttering under their breath, "There goes that building."

Instantly I responded, "Don't worry. All the money that we need is in the house!" Recalling what the Holy Spirit had told me the day before, I announced, "I need three people who can give $10,000 to stand up." Within a split second, three people stood. I then said, "I need five people who can give $5,000 to stand." Instantly five people stood. This process continued for another ten minutes. In less than fifteen minutes, we had $100,000 cash. The place erupted with praise and shouts because we saw firsthand the power of corporate faith and what can happen when people unite together in a single mission. After we moved in, we later learned that our facility was a famous building in American church history. It was built for Rev. Dr. Harry Emerson Fosdick, a world-renowned theologian. Our 1994 purchase of this Romanesque cathedral generated a lot of media attention including an extensive article by the *New York Times*.[1]

How can we as a Christian community attain God's promises and accomplish his purposes for our lives? Whatever God's purpose for a particular local congregation or denomination, it will require some corporate steps of faith. If the vision of a people requires little faith and commitment from its members, you have to wonder if that is really God's purpose and calling. God calls us to do things that we could never do on our own without his help. In this way his kingdom expands, and so does our faith.

The writer of Hebrews exhorted his readers with these words:

> Let us hold unswervingly to the hope we profess, for he who promised is faithful. And let us consider how we may

spur one another on toward love and good deeds. Let us not give up meeting together, as some are in the habit of doing, but let us encourage one another—and all the more as you see the Day approaching.

Hebrews 10:23–25

An effective method of meditating on God's Word is to paraphrase a verse in your own words. Here is how I would paraphrase the verse above:

You've gone through some very difficult times, and it may not be over yet. But whatever happens, don't give up hope, because God will prove himself faithful to you. Since we're all going through difficult times, think about how we can encourage one another. And when things get really bad, resist the temptation to isolate yourself. Get together with some other believers so that you can be encouraged.

My own personal salvation is synonymous to the deliverance from Egypt. Jesus Christ saved me from my own bondage to sin. However, God's intention was also to take me not just from sin to salvation but from isolation to fellowship with the whole people of God. I don't want to be like the children of Israel who let their fears and doubts hinder them from attaining to the fullness of God's plan and purpose for their lives.

So my prayer is this: *God, help me to be not just a good starter but also a good finisher. And I don't want to finish by myself; I want to finish with those I began the race with and others who have come to journey with me over time. My goal*

is not only to accomplish your purpose for my life but to par-
ticipate in the purpose you have for us together as a Christian
community, and that too is the focus of my faith. In Jesus's
name. Amen.

ten

KEEPING HOPE ALIVE

E very now and then, some unexplainable situation
occurs in each of our lives, causing us to reevaluate
faith, life's meaning, and the priorities we want to live
by. On September 11, 2001, all of America, especially those
of us who live on the East Coast, became brutally aware of
the brevity of life. The terrorist attack against our nation
prompted immediate changes in our perspective on family,
God, national appreciation, and the value of freedom.

When tragedy strikes on either a personal or societal
level, typically the first thing victims talk about is how it
has helped them realize what is really important in their
lives. Suddenly the perspective of faith takes on a deeper,
more lasting change. One begins to see faith from a higher

vantage point. Faith now is not just to be used to acquire things but to preserve a good life, both on an individual level and on a societal level. This dimension of faith helps us to keep hope alive.

The Importance of Hope

The apostle Paul wrote, "Now we see but a poor reflection as in a mirror; then we shall see face to face. Now I know in part; then I shall know fully, even as I am fully known. And now these three remain: faith, hope and love. But the greatest of these is love" (1 Cor. 13:12–13). The Christians in Corinth were so focused on aspects of life, ministry, and church order (or disorder) that Paul had to point out that they were missing things of eternal significance.

The Corinthian Christians were debating issues such as gifts of the Spirit, leadership, communion, and church order. Paul affirmed the importance of these issues but reminded them to discern the difference between things temporal and things eternal. He made his point by saying that when the Lord returns and we enter the eternal state, all the things they were arguing about will become irrelevant. All our hair-splitting over minor theological issues today will pass away. However, *faith, hope*, and *love* are the eternal constants in this life that will remain after all else is gone (cf. 1 Cor. 13:13).

In one sense, faith, hope, and love are inseparable qualities. It has always seemed to me, however, that hope is different from the other two virtues. Faith and love are precisely defined and integrated into our systematic theology. Specific types of love are designated by the Greek words *agape* (self-

174

less love), *philia* (friendship, brotherly love), and *eros* (erotic love). Also, God's love for us is demonstrated in concrete ways. Faith is also defined with great precision, and we talk about the content of our faith in great detail.

What then is *hope*, precisely, and what place does it have in our theology and in practical Christian living? We generally consider one who has faith to also have hope, and vice versa. However, in rare situations when faith and hope are under extreme heat and pressure, we usually discover that in people whose faith is almost gone, still a faint glimmer of hope remains. If you've never been in that situation, you might wonder how you can have hope in God's plan and provision while at the same time feel unsure about what to believe. If, however, you are one of those people who is or has been in that situation, you know exactly what I mean. You hang on to hope when faith no longer makes any sense.

Let's examine three characteristics of hope: (1) Hope provides patience with paradox, (2) hope shapes perspective, and (3) hope opens the door to God's grace.

Hope Provides Patience with Paradox

Faith usually has clear focus and direction. We pray and believe for specific things. Sometimes we need to be very specific about our prayers. However, when you come to the place where you no longer know what to pray for or what to believe, when your life is dominated by contradiction and paradox, what you hang on to is hope. Hope sustains you when nothing else makes sense and there seems to be no rhyme or reason to the circumstances of your life. The first characteristic of hope, therefore, is that it provides you with the patience to endure the unexplainable paradoxes of life that you and I may never understand.

As a young believer, I assumed that really mature Christians were the ones who had a perfect answer for every circumstance of life and for every theological question. That, to me, was great faith. Over time, however, I've come to realize that the very opposite is true. The most mature Christians, doctrinally and behaviorally, are those who hang on to two biblical ideas that seem completely contradictory, and do it very comfortably: They affirm the unalterable sovereignty of God while recognizing the reality of free will; they believe in the Trinity and at the same time say that there is one God. They seem to have learned why Paul could marvel,

> Oh, the depth of the riches of the wisdom and knowledge
> of God!
> How unsearchable are his judgments,
> and his paths beyond tracing out! . . .
> For from him and through him and to him are all things.
> To him be glory forever! Amen.
> Romans 11:33, 36

Paul understood that many things about God are beyond our ability to understand. There was room for a great deal of mystery in his theology.

On the other hand, those who cannot endure the slightest paradox formulate their battle plans and are ready to argue at a moment's notice. Their theological arguments are in fact evidence of immaturity and small thinking about God.

Many believers have come to the place where it seems everything they believe in has fallen apart. They've come to the place where their faith and experience seem to be in total contradiction. People in that situation often dread seeing their Christian friends and talking about their problems. You may have reached this point—when the available evidence seems to suggest that faith has not worked, and all the clichés commonly used to encourage believers seem inadequate and inappropriate. At such times, it's hard to explain your situation to others. If it doesn't make sense to you, how could you make them understand?

That was the situation for the Bible's classic sufferer, Job. Things had gone so badly for so long that the obvious conclusion was that God had forsaken him. Yet while Job struggled with faith, he clung stubbornly to hope, saying, "Though he slay me, yet will I *hope* in him" (Job 13:15, emphasis added).

As with Job, when it comes to practical Christian living, those who are mature in their walk with the Lord look at tragedy and unfulfilled expectations in their lives and boldly declare that God loves them, is for them, and is completely faithful to them. There may be too many glaring contradictions between their faith and their experience for them even to begin to explain it, but they have hung on to God, as did Abraham, hoping against hope when things seemed impossible.

Sometimes those contradictions get resolved in this life, and sometimes they do not. Even in the case of the models of faith in Hebrews 11, many of them "were still living by faith when they died" and "did not receive the things promised" (v. 13). They trusted that in some way God would turn that glimmer of hope into an inner confidence and a peace that transcends understanding regardless of the outcome.

Because hope transcends the unexplainable paradoxes of life, it is consequently the greatest and highest expression of faith. Do you want to grow in faith and in maturity in your walk with the Lord? If so, then somewhere along the way you will have to let hope sustain you through unexplainable contradictions. It is an experience that every great person of faith listed in Hebrews 11 went through.

In this life there will not always be a fairy-tale ending that resolves all contradictions and answers all questions. Yet you can be absolutely sure that at the coming of the Lord and the judgment, God will through Jesus "reconcile to himself all things" (Col. 1:20). Every event of this life will be understood in light of God's plan and purpose. And every deed will be reconciled to his perfect righteousness and justice—despite the fact that in this life we will see injustice and tragic circumstances, some even happening to us.

We do a great disservice to potential converts and to new Christians by pretending this is otherwise, overselling Christianity as a pat scheme by which all things will work out nicely and neatly for Christians. In an eternal sense, yes! In this earthly life, it happens often, but not always.

Hope Shapes Perspective

The second characteristic of hope is that it informs, shapes, and changes your perspective. The quest for perspective in recent years is reflected in the flood of mission statements and lists of core values emerging from corporate boardrooms. Today that same process has filtered down to managers, homemakers, blue-collar workers, and even high school students. Formulating a personal mission-and-values statement is a trendy thing to do.

This trend seems to be driven not just by the high demand on people's time but by the extraordinary list of things to do, places to go, things to see, ways to serve, games to play, and causes to support. Corporations seek to define their purpose and values because, with the complexity of the business environment and the size and diversity of their organization, it is easy to lose sight of the most important things. Today, the same thing is true for individuals.

Unfortunately, many such core values statements and strategic planning documents typically get put into a nice binder that collects dust on the shelf. It is one thing to define your perspective but quite another to maintain that perspective throughout the daily grind of business or everyday life.

This chapter opened with a reference to how tragedy, death, and near-death experiences change one's values and perspective. However, as time passes, the effect often diminishes, and eventually that heightened awareness fades. Wouldn't it be great to live your whole life with the kind of perspective you had at that moment when your values were eternally assessed? No one wants post-trauma routine to get them into a situation in which all they have to hang on to is a slender thread of hope. If we do reach that point, our natural response is to cry out to God, "Why did you allow this to happen?"

The answers to those kinds of questions are not easy. In fact, it's often impossible to know the mind of God regarding specific reasons behind tragedy. I do know, however, that in situations in which you are reduced to hope, you can always learn a lesson about values and perspective. And maybe that's what God was trying to teach you all along.

Trials are like fire to our perspective. They burn away temporal things, while only the truly valuable things remain. Our perspective and sense of values determine how we view the difficulties of life.

Dr. Viktor Frankl was a psychiatrist imprisoned in a Nazi concentration camp in Germany during World War II. His wife was killed, and he was regularly beaten for his faith. After he came out of prison, he wrote his famous book entitled *Man's Search for Meaning*.

Dr. Frankl shares the story of an elderly physician who came to him for counseling. This man was depressed because his wife of many years had died, and he didn't know how to function without her. Dr. Frankl asked the grieving widower, "What would have happened, Doctor, if you had died first, and your wife would have had to survive you?" The man said if that had happened, she would have been overcome with grief and depression. He doubted that she would have been able to function. Frankl told the man that he ought to be thankful, because his wife was spared that grief. The doctor's gift, Frankl suggested, was outlasting and outliving his wife. That statement changed the grieving widower's perspective.[1]

When the journey of faith moves you into a dimension where only hope can survive, choose the perspective that hope offers, and live . . . *live!*

Hope Opens the Door to God's Grace

The third characteristic of hope is that it endures when your faith and experience seem to be at odds with one another.

In his second letter to the Corinthian church, the apostle Paul refers to his "thorn in the flesh." No one ever had a more dramatic conversion experience than Paul when he encountered the risen Lord on the Damascus Road. Subsequently, he also had been miraculously delivered from prisons, storms, and mobs. He had through the power of the Holy Spirit performed astounding miracles, healed the sick, and even raised the dead. He himself had been raised up after being left for dead from a stoning in Galatia.

But despite all these victories there was one setback—the so-called thorn in his flesh. There are many theories among Bible scholars about what this "thorn" was. Some say it was a disease of the eyes. Others think it was demonic oppression or persecution from Jewish leaders. In any case, Paul writes, "Three times I pleaded with the Lord to take it away from me" (2 Cor. 12:8). It was a prayer that never seemed to be answered. Finally the Lord spoke to him on the matter, saying, "My grace is sufficient for you, for my power is made perfect in weakness" (2 Cor. 12:9).

Hopeless situations are an opportunity in disguise for a greater measure of God's grace and power to be released in your life. This dimension of grace is far deeper than many Christians' narrow understanding of the term. When asked to define *grace*, the most common answer has to do with "unmerited favor." That is indeed a true definition, but it leaves hidden the depths and power of grace. *Grace is the power of God working in and through you, enabling you to do what you could never do and to be what you could never be.*

Saul of Tarsus, a bigoted Jew, the chief persecutor of the church, a bald-headed little man (by tradition) with a thorn in the flesh, became the apostle Paul, one of the most influential figures in Western civilization. How did he do that? John Wesley called it "gracious ability."

Notice Paul's own definition of grace: "By the grace of God I am what I am, and his grace to me was not without effect. No, I worked harder than all of them [the other apostles]—yet not I, but the grace of God that was with me" (1 Cor. 15:10). Paul's "thorn in the flesh" seemed to be a contradiction to this outpouring of grace. Yet it was a part of what spurred Paul to do what God called him to do.

Sometimes the contradictions in our own lives precipitate the question, "God, if you have called me to serve you in this way, then why haven't you fixed the problems, opened the doors, removed the obstacles, supplied the needs?" How could it be that God would make it harder rather than easier for you to do his work? That makes no sense.

Or does it? Paul had the same persistent question, until finally the Lord revealed to him that his ministry would *not* be easier without his thorn in the flesh. The reason was because God's power would be perfected in Paul's difficulty. Paul had to depend on grace, something those endowed with great abilities and easy pathways often have a hard time doing.

With that understanding, Paul's perspective changed. Instead of agonizing over the paradox, trying to cover up his personal problems, or even pretending that the problem would go away, Paul fully embraced the contradiction. He goes on in the Corinthian letter to say, "Therefore I will boast all the more gladly about my weaknesses. . . . For when I am weak, then I am strong" (2 Cor. 12:9–10).

You can detect in Paul's letter that he was at perfect peace with God's "No." His perspective is a good illustration of the definition of faith in Hebrews 11:1 we have frequently noted: "Now faith is being sure of what we hope for and certain of what we do not see." You could also add, "being certain of what we do not understand." It sounds unreasonable, illogical, and oxymoronic, but hope enables you to be at peace with unexplainable contradictions, immovable obstacles, and even unanswered prayers.

A relationship with God is more than simply obeying rules and regulations; it's even more than knowing how to utilize the mechanics of faith. A relationship with God is more than trying to systematically reduce prayer and faith to pat formulas. There is not always an immediate and discernible cause-effect relationship between every problem and a lack of faith. The "laws" of faith cannot be equated with natural laws such as gravity or buoyancy.

Even when we dive into the depths of these natural laws, we find paradoxes and contradictions, because principles are at work beyond our surface understanding. Similarly, as we go deeper and deeper with God, we eventually run into issues we don't understand. That's what caused David to write, "Why are you downcast, O my soul? Why so disturbed within me? Put your hope in God" (Ps. 42:5).

If you can place your hope in God, you can become, like David, a person who pursues God's *heart* and not just

God's *resources*. And that is how your faith, hope, and love are perfected.

Epilogue

We began this journey together by examining Hebrews 11—action, excitement, and powerful praise reports that declare how historical characters exercised their faith in God. It is human nature, however, to focus on the exciting outcome while ignoring the arduous journey of their faith.

You may have just overcome one trial by exercising your faith, and now another one has surfaced. What are you to do? This book has equipped you to exercise authentic faith to appropriate all of God's promises and provision. Even if your situation has threatened your faith, I trust you have seen how you can be empowered with *hope* and thus stand strong in the midst of the storm.

In most cases, authentic faith is all that is needed to bring deliverance and provision. Remember Jesus's word to Peter in response to his request to join Jesus on the water: "Come!"

It's your time now to walk on the water. Go ahead! Step out of the boat and enjoy your walk of faith!

NOTES

Introduction

1. Sermon Notes, "Illustration on Perseverance," http://www.sermonnotes.com/members/deluxe/illus/p.htm (accessed October 2003).

Chapter 1: The Day before the Miracles

1. Gerhard Kittel, *Theological Dictionary of the New Testament*, vol. 2 (Grand Rapids: Eerdmans, 1976), 476.

2. Charles Haddon Spurgeon, *Spurgeon's Sermons*, vol. 3 (Grand Rapids: Baker, 1883), 261.

3. Norman Vincent Peale, *The Power of Positive Thinking* (Pawling, NY: Foundation for Christian Living, 1978), 1.

Chapter 3: The Journey of Faith Defined

1. F. F. Bruce, *The New International Commentary on the New Testament: The Epistle to the Hebrews* (Grand Rapids: Eerdmans, 1964), 278.

2. See also 2 Corinthians 1:22–23; 5:5.

3. Norman Grubb, *Rees Howells: Intercessor* (Fort Washington, PA: Christian Literature Crusade, 1996), 85.

4. W. E. Vine, *Vine's Expository Dictionary of Old and New Testament Words*, vol. 4 (Iowa Falls, IA: Riverside, 1971), 88.

5. Charles G. Finney, *Revivals of Religion* (Grand Rapids: Revell, 1993), 264.

Chapter 4: Cultivating Authentic Faith

1. Francis A. Schaeffer, *How Should We Then Live?* (Wheaton: Crossway, 1983), 55.

2. Ronald H. Nash, *Worldviews in Conflict* (Grand Rapids: Zondervan, 1992), 55.

3. W. Bingham Hunter, quoted in Lee Stroebel, *The Case for Faith* (Grand Rapids: Zondervan, 2000), 11.

4. Lisa Beamer, *Let's Roll!* (Wheaton: Tyndale, 2002), 10.

Chapter 5: Storms Offer Lessons in Faith

1. Corrie ten Boom, *Tramp for the Lord* (New York: Jove, 1978), 86.

Chapter 6: Riding Out the Storms of Life

1. David D. Ireland, *Failure Is Written in Pencil* (Verona, NJ: Impact, 2000), 52.

2. James S. Hewett, ed., *Illustrations Unlimited* (Wheaton: Tyndale, 1988), 205.

3. Paul Lee Tan, *Encyclopedia of 7,700 Illustrations*, Logos Bible Software (Garland, TX: Bible Communications, 1996).

Chapter 7: How to Apply Faith

1. C. G. Finney, *Revivals of Religion* (Grand Rapids: Revell, 1993), 98.

2. E. M. Bounds, *Purpose in Prayer* (Grand Rapids: Baker, 1920), 53.

3. R. D. Chatham, *Fasting: A Biblical Historical Study* (South Plainfield, NJ: Bridge, 1987), xvii.

4. A. W. Tozer, *The Pursuit of God* (Camp Hill, PA: Christian Publications, 1982), 83.

Chapter 8: Five Enemies of Faith

1. Arthur F. Lenehan, *The Best of Bits & Pieces* (Fairfield, NJ: Economics Press), 74.

2. Tan, *Encyclopedia of 7,700 Illustrations.*

3. Sermon Notes, "Jesus' Formula for Success," http://www.sermonnotes.com/members/deluxe/sermons/mk8v34.htm (accessed October 2003).

4. Jim Cymbala, *Fresh Faith* (Grand Rapids: Zondervan, 1999), 104.

Chapter 9: Faith Does Not Stand Alone

1. Gustav Niebuhr, "A Tale of Two Congregations," *New York Times,* August 1, 1994, sec. B.

Chapter 10: Keeping Hope Alive

1. Viktor E. Frankl, *Man's Search for Meaning* (New York: Simon & Schuster, 1984), 135.

David D. Ireland, Ph.D., can be heard nationwide on a daily radio and weekly television show, *IMPACT with David Ireland*. In 1986 he planted Christ Church of Montclair, New Jersey, with six people—it has since grown to five thousand active members. He holds an undergraduate degree in mechanical engineering (Farleigh Dickinson University), graduate degrees in civil engineering (Stevens Institute of Technology) and theology (Alliance Theological Seminary), along with an earned Ph.D. in organizational leadership (Regent University). He and his wife, Marlinda, have been married for over twenty years.